Bacterium in Broth

CRIMINAL JUSTICE, LAW ENFORCEMENT AND CORRECTIONS

NOT SO NICE

GIRLS' DELINQUENCY ISSUES

CRIMINAL JUSTICE, LAW ENFORCEMENT AND CORRECTIONS

Selective Prosecution in the
Federal Criminal Justice System?
Kevin H. Mabe (Editor)
2010. ISBN: 978-1-60692-684-0

Police and Augmented
Reality Technology
Matthew D. Blount (Editor)
2010. ISBN: 978-1-60692-206-4

Police Guide for Responding
to People with Mental Illness
Kjell Grönberg (Editor)
2010. ISBN: 978-1-60741-479-7

Mass Marketing and Consumer
Fraud: Background,
Issues and Data
Martin A. Parham (Editor)
2010. ISBN: 978-1-60692-793-9

Guidelines for Domestic
FBI Operations
Carlo Bianchi (Editor)
2010. ISBN: 978-1-60692-798-4

Police Management:
Professional Integrity in Policing
Petter Gottschalk
2010. ISBN: 978-1-60876-903-2

Digital Evidence
in the Courtroom
John D. Nilsson (Editor)
2010. ISBN: 978-1-60741-803-0

Organized Crime in the U.S.
Wesley B. Knowles (Editor)
2010. ISBN: 978-1-60741-524-4

Revisiting the Social Contract:
Community Justice
and Public Safety
*Kathleen Auerhahn
and Caitlin J. McGuire*
2010. ISBN: 978-1-60876-446-4

Domestic Violence:
Law Enforcement
Response and Legal Perspectives
Mario R. Dewalt (Editor)
2010. ISBN: 978-1-60876-774-8

White-Collar Criminals:
Theoretical and Managerial
Perspectives of Financial Crime
Peter Gottschalk
2010. ISBN: 978-1-61668-775-5
2010. ISBN: 978-1-61728-639-1
(E-book)

The Prison System
and its Effects - Wherefrom,
Whereto, and Why?
Antony Taylor
2010. ISBN: 978-1-61728-035-1
2010. ISBN: 978-1-61728-324-6
(E-book)

Perspectives
on Juvenile Offenders
Owen B. Hahn (Editor)
2010. ISBN: 978-1-60876-819-6

Not So Nice:
Girls' Delinquency Issues
Adam P. Mawer (Editor)
2010. ISBN: 978-1-60876-268-2

CRIMINAL JUSTICE, LAW ENFORCEMENT AND CORRECTIONS

NOT SO NICE

GIRLS' DELINQUENCY ISSUES

ADAM P. MAWER
EDITOR

Nova Science Publishers, Inc.
New York

NOTICE TO THE READER

The Publisher has taken reasonable care in the preparation of this book, but makes no expressed or implied warranty of any kind and assumes no responsibility for any errors or omissions. No liability is assumed for incidental or consequential damages in connection with or arising out of information contained in this book. The Publisher shall not be liable for any special, consequential, or exemplary damages resulting, in whole or in part, from the readers' use of, or reliance upon, this material. Any parts of this book based on government reports are so indicated and copyright is claimed for those parts to the extent applicable to compilations of such works.

Independent verification should be sought for any data, advice or recommendations contained in this book. In addition, no responsibility is assumed by the publisher for any injury and/or damage to persons or property arising from any methods, products, instructions, ideas or otherwise contained in this publication.

This publication is designed to provide accurate and authoritative information with regard to the subject matter covered herein. It is sold with the clear understanding that the Publisher is not engaged in rendering legal or any other professional services. If legal or any other expert assistance is required, the services of a competent person should be sought. FROM A DECLARATION OF PARTICIPANTS JOINTLY ADOPTED BY A COMMITTEE OF THE AMERICAN BAR ASSOCIATION AND A COMMITTEE OF PUBLISHERS.

LIBRARY OF CONGRESS CATALOGING-IN-PUBLICATION DATA

Not so nice : girls' delinquency issues / editor, Adam P. Mawer.
  p. cm.
 Includes index.
 ISBN 978-1-60876-268-2 (hardcover)
 1. Female juvenile delinquents--United States. 2. Juvenile justice, Administration of--United States. 3. Juvenile delinquency--United States. I. Mawer, Adam P.
 HV9104.N68 2010
 364.36082'0973--dc22

2009049871

Published by Nova Science Publishers, Inc. ✦ *New York*

CONTENTS

PREFACE

Girls' delinquency has attracted the attention of federal, state, and local policymakers for more than a decade as girls have increasingly become involved in the juvenile justice system. For girls, the key risk factors for delinquency and incarceration are family dysfunction, trauma and sexual abuse, mental health and substance abuse problems, high-risk sexual behaviors, school problems and affiliation with deviant peers. The authors of this book examine the developmental sequences of girls' delinquent behavior, as well as the factors that protect girls against delinquency. In addition, issues such as patterns of offending among adolescents are explored and how they differ for girls and boys. The causes and correlates of girls' delinquency are discussed as well. This book consists of public documents which have been located, gathered, combined, reformatted, and enhanced with a subject index, selectively edited and bound to provide easy access.

Chapter 1 - Juvenile delinquency can become a pathway to adult offending. Delin- quency experts search for ways to counter delinquency before it starts, providing intervention for juveniles in high-risk situations—such as those with severe economic disadvantages or living in high-crime neighborhoods.

However, the majority of juveniles arrested are male, which means that a good deal of research on juvenile delinquents has been performed on a mostly male population that does not account for girls' and boys' differences. Despite much research on the causes of boys' delinquency, few studies have examined which girls become delinquent or why. Additionally, intervention and treat- ment programs have been traditionally designed with boys in mind, and little is known about how well girls respond to these interventions.

In the 1990s, a surge of girls' arrests brought female juvenile crimes to the country's attention. Girls' rates of arrest for some crimes increased faster than boys' rates of arrest. By 2004, girls accounted for 30 percent of all juvenile arrests, but delinquency experts did not know whether these trends reflected changes in girls' behavior or changes in arrest patterns. The juvenile justice field was struggling to understand how best to respond to the needs of the girls entering the system.

To determine the reason behind these increasing arrest rates, the Office of Juvenile Justice and Delinquency Prevention (OJJDP) convened the Girls Study Group (see "About the Girls Study Group"). The group sponsored a series of studies to gain a better understanding of girls' involvement in delinquency and guide the development, testing, and dissemination of strategies that would reduce incidents of delinquency and violence among girls.

Chapter 2 - This report provides a statistical profile of female juvenile offenders in Hawaii. It utilizes two main datasets: (1) CY 2004 Juvenile Justice Information System data; and (2) Family Court case file information on juvenile offenders who were either on probation or incarcerated at the Hawaii Youth Correctional Facility (HYCF). The report first examines general trends in juvenile arrests and adjudications, focusing on gender and racial/ethnic differences in each category. It then analyzes gender differences in the social, psychological, family, drug use, and academic backgrounds in the case file sample. Finally, the report examines intragender differences between HYCF girls and non-HYCF girls.

Chapter 3 features a letter to the U. S. House of Representatives.

Chapter 4 - According to data from the Federal Bureau of Investigation, from 1991 to 2000, arrests of girls increased more (or decreased less) than arrests of boys for most types of offenses. By 2004, girls accounted for 30 percent of all juvenile arrests. However, questions remain about whether these trends reflect an actual increase in girls' delinquency or changes in societal responses to girls' behavior. To find answers to these questions, the Office of Juvenile Justice and Delinquency Prevention (OJJDP) convened the Girls Study Group to establish a theoretical and empirical foundation to guide the development, testing, and dissemination of strategies to reduce or prevent girls' involvement in delinquency and violence.

Chapter 5 - According to data from the Federal Bureau of Investigation, from 1991 to 2000, arrests of girls increased more (or decreased less) than arrests of boys for most types of offenses. By 2004, girls accounted for 30 percent of all juvenile arrests. However, questions remain about whether these trends reflect an actual increase in girls' delinquency or changes in societal responses to girls' behavior. To find answers to these questions, the Office of Juvenile Justice and Delinquency Prevention (OJJDP) convened the Girls Study Group to establish a theoretical and empirical foundation to guide the development, testing, and dissemination of strategies to reduce or prevent girls' involvement in delinquency and violence.

In: Not So Nice: Girls' Delinquency Issues   ISBN: 978-1-60876-268-2
Editor: Adam P. Mawer   © 2010 Nova Science Publishers, Inc.

Chapter 1

THE GIRLS STUDY GROUP - CHARTING THE WAY TO DELINQUENCY PREVENTION FOR GIRLS[*]

Margaret A. Zahn, Stephanie R. Hawkins, Janet Chiancone and Ariel Whitworth

Juvenile delinquency can become a pathway to adult offending. Delinquency experts search for ways to counter delinquency before it starts, providing intervention for juveniles in high-risk situations—such as those with severe economic disadvantages or living in high-crime neighborhoods.

However, the majority of juveniles arrested are male, which means that a good deal of research on juvenile delinquents has been performed on a mostly male population that does not account for girls' and boys' differences. Despite much research on the causes of boys' delinquency, few studies have examined which girls become delinquent or why. Additionally, intervention and treatment programs have been traditionally designed with boys in mind, and little is known about how well girls respond to these interventions.

In the 1990s, a surge of girls' arrests brought female juvenile crimes to the country's attention. Girls' rates of arrest for some crimes increased faster than boys' rates of arrest. By 2004, girls accounted for 30 percent of all juvenile

---

[*] This is an edited, reformatted and augmented version of a U. S. Department of Justice publication dated October 2008.

arrests, but delinquency experts did not know whether these trends reflected changes in girls' behavior or changes in arrest patterns. The juvenile justice field was struggling to understand how best to respond to the needs of the girls entering the system.

To determine the reason behind these increasing arrest rates, the Office of Juvenile Justice and Delinquency Prevention (OJJDP) convened the Girls Study Group (see "About the Girls Study Group"). The group sponsored a series of studies to gain a better understanding of girls' involvement in delinquency and guide the development, testing, and dissemination of strategies that would reduce incidents of delinquency and violence among girls.

The Girls Study Group (GSG) wanted to know—

- Which girls become delinquent?
- What factors protect girls from delinquency?
- What factors put girls at risk for delinquency?
- What pathways lead to girls' delinquency?
- What programs are most effective in preventing girls' delinquency?
- How should the criminal justice system respond to girls' delinquency?

The series of studies outlined in this Bulletin describe the ways in which the group worked to understand and respond to girls' delinquency. Using a combination of literature reviews, dataset analysis, and program and instrument reviews, they conducted a series of studies (each outlined in detail in forthcoming OJJDP Bulletins). These studies should shed light on why girls become delinquent, and provide a research foundation for the juvenile justice community to consider what treatment and intervention programs are most effective for girls. These studies include:

1. **Violence by Teenage Girls: Trends and Context.** This Bulletin describes recent trends in girls' offending and examines the settings in which girls commit crimes.

2. **Causes and Correlates of Girls' Delinquency.** This Bulletin examines the personal, family, peer, school, and community factors that can lead to delinquency.

3. **Resilient Girls—Factors that Protect Against Delinquency.** This Bulletin examines whether four factors—a caring adult, school

connectedness, school success, and religiosity—can protect girls from delinquency.

4. **Suitability of Assessment Instruments for Delinquent Girls.** This Bulletin determines whether current risk-assessment and treatment-focused instruments are appropriate for use with girls. It also provides guidance to practitioners on how to select instruments for use.

5. **Girls' Delinquency Programs— An Evidence-Based Review.** This Bulletin reviews girls' delinquency programs and determines whether they effectively intervene in delinquency trajectories.

6. **Developmental Sequences of Girls' Delinquent Behavior.** This Bulletin investigates the different patterns of delinquent behaviors that girls become involved in, and provides insight into the life pathways that lead to girls' delinquent behavior.

This document will provide highlights of the findings that are outlined in detail in the Bulletins described above. Most are forthcoming and will be available through the Juvenile Justice Clearinghouse (http://www. fsu.edu/~crimdo/jjclearinghouse/ jjclearinghouse.html) and published on the OJJDP (http://ojjdp.ncjrs. org) and Girls Study Group (http:/ / girlsstudygroup.rti.org) Web sites.

GIRLS STUDY GROUP MEMBERS

Dr. Margaret A. Zahn, Principal Investigator, Girls Study Group (2004–March 2008) Senior Research Scientist, RTI International; Professor, North Carolina State University

Dr. Stephanie R. Hawkins, Principal Investigator, Girls Study Group (April 2008–Present)
Research Clinical Psychologist, RTI International

Dr. Robert Agnew, Professor, Department of Sociology, Emory University

Dr. Elizabeth Cauffman, Assistant Professor, Department of Psychology and Social Behavior, University of California–Irvine

Dr. Meda Chesney-Lind, Professor, Women's Studies Program, University of Hawaii–Manoa

Dr. Gayle Dakof, Associate Research Professor, Department of Epidemiology and Public Health, University of Miami

Dr. Del Elliott, Director, Center for the Study and Prevention of Violence, University of Colorado
Dr. Barry Feld, Professor, School of Law, University of Minnesota

Dr. Diana Fishbein, Director, Transdisciplinary Behavioral Science Program, RTI International

Dr. Peggy Giordano, Professor of Sociology, Center for Family and Demographic Research, Bowling Green State University

Dr. Candace Kruttschnitt, Professor, Department of Sociology, University of Minnesota

Dr. Jody Miller, Associate Professor, Department of Criminology and Criminal Justice, University of Missouri–St. Louis

Dr. Merry Morash, Professor, School of Criminal Justice, Michigan State University

Dr. Darrell Steffensmeier, Professor, Department of Sociology, Pennsylvania State University

Ms. Giovanna Taormina, Executive Director, Girls Circle Association

Dr. Donna-Marie Winn, Senior Research Scientist, Center for Social Demography and Ethnography, Duke University

VIOLENCE BY TEENAGE GIRLS: TRENDS AND CONTEXT

The upswing in girls' violence in the late 20th century had many people in the juvenile justice community concerned. They wanted to know what factors influenced girls' offending, and what kinds of programs and policies could reduce girls' violence.

To answer these questions, OJJDP convened the Girls Study Group. The Group's initial research project examined rates of girls' arrests, delinquency, and victimization. Researchers examined arrest data from the FBI's Uniform Crime Reports, delinquency surveys from the Monitoring the Future study, and victimization surveys from the Bureau of Justice Statistics' National Crime Victimization Survey.

This research resulted in the *Trends and Context* Bulletin, which provides answers to a number of questions:

How have girls' and boys' arrest rates increased in the past decade?

- Girls account for a smaller proportion of overall juvenile arrests than boys, but arrest patterns for both groups have diverged over the past decade. Between 1996 and 2005, overall arrests decreased for both groups. However, this decrease was greater for boys than girls.
- Notably, between 1996 and 2005, girls' arrests for simple assault increased 24 percent.

Are girls actually committing more crimes?

- Despite increasing arrest rates in the past decade, self-report data suggest that girls' behavior has not changed. In fact, self-report data suggest girls' and boys' assault rates have dropped in recent years.

What would explain the increasing arrest rates for girls?

Arrest laws and changes in law enforcement policy appear to have had more of an impact on arrest rates than changes in girls' behavior. Possible explanations for this include:

- Changes in local law enforcement policies that lowered the threshold for reporting assaults or classifying assaults as aggravated.

- Some status offenses involving a domestic dispute between a girl and her parent or sibling could now be classified as simple assault and could result in arrest. This sort of arrest is an unintended consequence of "mandatory arrest" laws in cases of domestic violence.
- Schools' zero-tolerance policies toward youth violence may have increased police referral for fights involving girls.

To test some of the possible explanations outlined above, the Girls Study Group conducted a special analysis that looked at local mandatory and pro-arrest policies to determine if there were indications that these had an impact on the increasing number of girls' arrests. Their findings indicate that mandatory and pro-arrest policies increased the likelihood of arrest for both girls and boys, but the effects appear stronger for girls. This may be explained by the fact that family conflict accounts for a larger proportion of girls' offending than of boys' offending.[1]

ABOUT THE GIRLS STUDY GROUP

In 2004, OJJDP convened the Girls Study Group, an interdisciplinary group of scholars and practitioners who would work together to develop a comprehensive research foundation for understanding and responding to girls' involvement in delinquency.

Through a competitive process, RTI International was selected to lead the Girls Study Group Project.

The group includes experts from the fields of sociology, psychology, criminology, and gender studies, as well as legal practitioners and girls' program development coordinators.

The Girls Study Group research consists of—

- Reviewing literature on girls' delinquency.
- Analyzing secondary datasets.
- Assessing programs that target female delinquents.
- Reviewing risk assessment and treatment-focused instruments for delinquent girls.

For more information about the Girls Study Group, see http://girlsstudygroup.rti.org.

CAUSES AND CORRELATES OF GIRLS' DELINQUENCY

Girls' delinquency has become an increasing dilemma in recent years, in part because of higher arrest rates, and in part because little research to date has focused on female juvenile delinquents. By 2004, females made up 25 percent of all juvenile arrests for aggravated assault, and 33 percent of juvenile arrests for other assaults. So why do some girls become delinquent? A great deal of research has examined the factors involved in male delinquency, but the factors involved in female delinquency remained largely unknown.

To understand the causes of female delinquency, the Girls Study Group reviewed more than 2,300 social science articles and book chapters that examine factors involved in delinquent behavior for girls ages 11 to 18. They also examined factors that protect girls from becoming delinquent. They found that while certain factors predict or prevent delinquency in both sexes, a number of factors influence girls' behavior more strongly than boys' behavior.

The factors that equally increase the risk of delinquency for both sexes include—

- The family's dynamics (i.e., how parents supervise and monitor a child, family history of criminal behavior, child maltreatment).
- A child's involvement in school.
- The neighborhood a child lives in (e.g., poverty level, crime rate, employment rate).
- The level of availability of community-based programs.

Some factors increase or decrease a girl's risk of delinquency more than a boy's, including—

- **Early puberty.** Early puberty increases girls' risk for delinquency, particularly if they come from disadvantaged neighborhoods and have dysfunctional families. This disparity between biological and social maturity can lead to increased conflict with parents or negative associations with older boys or men.

- **Sexual abuse or maltreatment.** Compared to boys, girls experience more sexual victimization overall, including sexual assaults, rapes, and sexual harassment. However, all types of maltreatment (sexual, physical, and neglect) can increase the risk of delinquency for both sexes.

- **Depression and anxiety.** Depression and anxiety disorders have been associated with delinquency. Girls receive these diagnoses more frequently than boys.

- **Romantic partners.** When a youth's boyfriend or girlfriend commits a crime, he or she may also engage in delinquent behavior. For less serious crimes, girls are influenced more by their boyfriends than boys by their girlfriends. For serious crimes, they are equally affected.

RESILIENT GIRLS—FACTORS THAT PROTECT AGAINST DELINQUENCY

Some children manage to achieve success despite the difficulties they encounter in life. This ability to positively adapt to negative situations is called resilience. Positive experiences in life can strengthen a child's ability to become resilient to the difficult situations—abuse, neglect, poverty, witnessing violence—that can lead to delinquency.

An investigation by the Girls Study Group examined whether experiencing protective factors during adolescence could keep girls from offending. These protective factors included—

- Support from a caring adult.
- Success in school—as measured by grade point average.
- School connectedness—a positive perception of the school environment and positive interactions with people at school.
- Religiosity—how important religion was to the girl.

The researchers analyzed self-report surveys from the National Longitudinal Study of Adolescent Health. They found:

- **Caring adult.** Girls who had a caring adult in their lives during adolescence were less likely to commit status or property offenses, sell drugs, join gangs, or commit simple or aggravated assault during adolescence. They also were less likely to commit simple assault as young adults.

- **School connectedness.** Girls who experienced school connectedness were not protected or at increased risk for delinquency during adolescence and young adulthood, with one exception—girls who experienced school connectedness during adolescence were more likely to become involved in aggravated assault in young adulthood.

- **School success.** Girls who experienced success in school during adolescence committed fewer status and property offenses and were less likely to join gangs in adolescence. School success helped protect them from involvement in simple and aggravated assault in adolescence and young adulthood. However, these girls were more likely to commit property offenses in young adulthood.

- **Religiosity.**[2] Girls who placed a high importance on religion during adolescence were less likely to sell drugs in early adolescence.

Researchers additionally examined the interaction between childhood risk factors and protective factors during adolescence on a child's propensity toward delinquent behavior. Although some of the protective factors helped girls not to engage in delinquent behavior, others could not mitigate the influence of risk factors that girls had endured since childhood. Their findings highlight the importance of considering girls' life histories when developing interventions for girls at high risk for delinquency.

SUITABILITY OF ASSESSMENT INSTRUMENTS FOR DELINQUENT GIRLS

When girls are arrested, referred to court for delinquent behavior, held in a secure facility, or released from confinement, juvenile justice practitioners need a way to examine the risks that these girls pose to those around them and the community at large. They also must determine how to identify the girls' treatment needs and make appropriate processing decisions (e.g., adjudication, detention).

Practitioners in the juvenile justice system typically use standardized instruments to make such decisions. These instruments help to systematize decisionmaking criteria across the juvenile justice system and make the decision process more consistent and objective. A number of instruments have been developed for screening and assessing at-risk and justice-involved youth, but many have not taken gender into consideration in their development.[3]

A group of researchers in the Girls Study Group reviewed 143 risk assessment and treatment-focused instruments, and examined whether they could appropriately determine youths' risks and needs. They wanted to know if the instruments had favorable gender-based performance, which includes—

- Gender-based instrument development (e.g., gender-specific items, scoring, or norms).
- Favorable gender-based analysis (e.g., research findings show it is equally effective for girls and boys).

The analysis examined instruments in four categories:

- Risk and risk/needs assessment instruments.
- Global needs assessment instruments.[4]
- Substance abuse instruments.
- Mental health instruments.

In this Bulletin, the authors list those instruments in each category with favorable gender-based performance. Overall, out of 143 instruments examined, 73 instruments had favorable gender-based performance. Of these 73 instruments, 28 offered gender-based instrument development, 25 had favorable gender-based analysis, and 20 met both criteria. The authors report that mental health instruments were most sensitive to gender differences. Many instruments did not have information on gender-based performance, and some were less favorable for girls.

Practitioners choosing an instrument for assessment in their community should consider the instrument's purpose, gender performance, cost, and local validation.

The Bulletin also provides detail on what practitioners should consider when selecting and administering instruments. It describes how to access further information about the many instruments reviewed.

GIRLS' DELINQUENCY PROGRAMS—
AN EVIDENCE-BASED REVIEW

Many States and communities design programs to prevent and treat female delinquency. However, researchers are unsure how effective these programs are. To examine how effectively these programs work, the Girls Study Group reviewed 26 promising and model programs in the Blueprints for Violence Prevention[5] database and completed a nationwide review of 61 girls' delinquency programs.

The research team reviewed the 61 girls' delinquency programs using the Office of Justice Programs' What Works Repository, and classified them based on evidence of their effectiveness. The classification framework that the authors used places programs in one of six levels of effectiveness:

- **Effective.** Effective programs have an experimental research design (i.e., a randomized controlled trial) that demonstrates a significant and sustained effect. The program should have been externally replicated at least once, with an implementation team and site separate from the original study.

- **Effective with reservation.** These programs have an experimental research design that demonstrates a significant and sustained effect. The program should have at least one successful replication. Reservations occur either because the program has only an internal replication, or because it has an external replication with modest results.

- **Promising.** These programs have either—
  - An experimental design without a successful replication.
  - A prospective, quasi-experimental research design (i.e., with no random assignment) that uses well-matched comparison groups. These programs have significant and sustained effects.

- **Inconclusive evidence.** These programs may have adequately rigorous research designs, but not sustained effects. Or they may have contradictory findings and not enough evidence demonstrating that the program is effective or ineffective.

- **Insufficient evidence.** These programs have a quasi-experimental design that lacks sufficient methodological rigor or a pre-post test design,[6] or involve a purely descriptive evaluation.[7]

- **Ineffective.** These programs have an experimental or quasi-experimental research design that failed to demonstrate a significant effect in an internal study or in a replication.

The nationwide review of girls' delinquency programs found that—

- Only 17 of the 61 programs cataloged had published evaluations.
- No programs could be rated effective, effective with reservation, or ineffective.
- Most programs could be rated as having insufficient evidence.

Two key findings from the review of girls' delinquency programs were that more evaluations are needed and many of these programs are no longer in existence, which suggests a lack of program sustainability.

The review of programs in the Blueprints for Violence Prevention database found that out of 26 promising and model programs, only 8 program evaluations analyzed whether program outcomes differed for boys and girls. However, 23 of these programs were equally effective for boys and girls. The programs targeted multiple risk factors for delinquency, had treatment plans that focused on the individual participant's needs, and developed connections between the program participants and resources in the community.[8]

DEVELOPMENTAL SEQUENCES OF GIRLS' DELINQUENT BEHAVIOR

As girls develop, their experiences and interactions impact their decisions and behavior. Some of these experiences and interactions may contribute to positive developmental outcomes and others may support involvement in negative behaviors.

The Girls Study Group explored the possibility that distinct developmental pathways could influence girls' delinquent behaviors. The resulting Bulletin may help researchers develop programs or policies that stop female delinquency before it starts.

To investigate the developmental pathways that lead to delinquency, the Girls Study Group analyzed data from two longitudinal studies of girls between ages 7 and 17—the Denver Youth Study,[9] which included 807 girls and the Fast Track Project,[10] which included 317 girls. The authors examined the lifetime prevalence of the types of delinquent behaviors forwhich girls were involved, including running away, truancy, public disorderliness, minor assault,[11] minor property offense, serious property offense, serious assault, drug sales, alcohol use, and drug use; and the developmental sequences of delinquent behavior followed by different groups of girls over the 7–17 age period.

The authors found that girls followed different developmental sequences. No one sequence or pathway of delinquent behaviors applied to a majority of girls. Additionally, a sizable proportion of girls were involved in delinquent offenses before middle school. Girls involved in more serious offending tended to return to a lower level of status or public disorder offending or returned to a nondelinquent status after a short time.

DISCUSSION

The research conducted by the Girls Study Group has yielded very important information for OJJDP and the juvenile justice field. Some of the findings have confirmed earlier research and anecdotal information, while other findings have contradicted many of the long-held beliefs about how girls become delinquent and how best to address their needs.

One of the first findings—and in some ways the most surprising finding—is that girls are not more violent than in previous years. The comparative analysis of official FBI data to self-report data revealed that, in fact, a change in how the juvenile justice system is responding to girls' behavior is largely responsible for the increased number of girls entering the system. Another surprising finding is that the increase in girls' arrests appears to be, in part, an unintended result of relatively new mandatory or pro-arrest policies put in place to protect victims of domestic violence. These are good policies, and necessary to protect victims. However, this unexpected outcome highlights the need to work with law enforcement to identify appropriate responses to conflict between girls and their family members, and for communities to support and provide families with access to family strengthening and mediation programs that provide intervention (rather than arrest).

Another key finding of the study group is that girls and boys experience many of the same delinquency risk factors. Although some risk factors are more gender sensitive, in general, focusing on general risk and protective factors for all youth seems a worthwhile effort. When it comes to providing intervention programming, some unique factors should be considered for girls. As with all delinquency prevention and intervention efforts, however, the focus should be on the individual youth and her specific needs and strengths. This is why using the appropriate risk assessment tools is important, whether the youth is a girl or a boy.

Perhaps the most significant finding of the Girls Study Group is that there continues to be a lack of reliable, accurate, and comprehensive information about good prevention and intervention programming for girls. Clearly, a concerted effort is needed to address the lack of evidence-based programs for the juvenile justice field, and the lack of programming for girls specifically. It is troubling that of all the girls' programs reviewed by the Girls Study Group, the majority of them were rated "insufficient" evidence and had not been evaluated to the degree that they could be considered "effective." More troubling is the fact that many of these programs do not have the resources to conduct rigorous evaluations.

In moving ahead, the Girls Study Group findings will provide OJJDP with the foundation needed to move ahead on a comprehensive program of information dissemination, training, technical assistance, and programming regarding girls' delinquency prevention and intervention. The findings of the group may assist States and communities in developing their own efforts to address girls' delinquency.

ACKNOWLEDGMENTS

Margaret A. Zahn was a Principal Scientist at RTI International and a professor at North Carolina State University during her Girls Study Group directorship, and is currently Acting Deputy Director of Research and Evaluation at the National Institute of Justice.

Stephanie R. Hawkins is a Research Clinical Psychologist with RTI International.

Janet Chiancone is a Research Coordinator at OJJDP.

Ariel Whitworth is a Communications Editor with the National Criminal Justice Reference Service.

End Notes

[1] Strom, K., T. Warner, L. Tichavsky, and M. Zahn (in development). Policing daughters: The role of domestic violence arrest policies in child-parent conflicts.

[2] Religiosity describes how important religion is to someone. In this study, answers to three questions—the frequency of praying, the frequency of attending religious events, and the girls' perception of the importance of religion—defined girls' religiosity.

[3] For instance, they may have been developed using a primarily male population.

[4] These instruments provide a broad-based assessment of areas that may need followup.

[5] See the Blueprints for Violence Prevention Web site at http:// www.colorado.edu/cspv/ blueprints/. The review of Blueprints for Violence Prevention programs was completed in July 2006. Updates to program ratings may have been added to the database since this date.

[6] A pre-post design measures program outcomes by comparing perceptions or behaviors at the end of a program (i.e., post- program) to some measurement before the program begins (i.e., pre-program).

[7] A purely descriptive design does not have rigorous methodology. The focus of descriptive research is to provide an accurate narrative of what is occurring.

[8] These connections can serve as a support mechanism for participants.

[9] For more information about the Denver Youth Study, see: http://ojjdp.ncjrs.org/programs/ ProgSummary.asp?pi=19 and http://www.casanet.org/library/ delinquency/youth-svy.htm.

[10] See the following three studies:

(1) Conduct Problems Prevention Research Group. 1992. A developmental and clinical model for the prevention of conduct disorders: The FAST Track program. *Development and Psychopathology* 4:509–527.

(2) Conduct Problems Prevention Research Group. 2000. Merging universal and indicated prevention programs: The Fast Track model. *Addictive Behaviors* 25:913–927.

(3) Conduct Problems Prevention Research Group. 2007. Fast Track randomized controlled trial to prevent externalizing psychiatric disorders: Findings from grades 3 to 9. *Journal of the American Academy of Child and Adolescent Psychiatry* 46:1250–1262.

[11] Denver Youth Study only.

In: Not So Nice: Girls' Delinquency Issues   ISBN: 978-1-60876-268-2
Editor: Adam P. Mawer   © 2010 Nova Science Publishers, Inc.

Chapter 2

THE FEMALE JUVENILE OFFENDER IN HAWAII*

Lisa J. Pasko

ACKNOWLEDGMENTS

This project would not have been possible without the support of the Juvenile Justice Information Committee's Subcommittee on Research. Special thanks to Senior Judge Frances Wong, First Circuit Family Court; Sharon Agnew, Executive Director, Office of Youth Services; Bonnie Brooks, Administrator, Second Circuit Family Court; Lawrence Mahuna, Chief of Police, Hawaii County; Donald Okashige, HYCF Business Services Supervisor; and Jay Kimura, Prosecuting Attorney, Hawaii County, for taking time to discuss the subject of this report and for helping whenever needed in the data collection efforts. Special thanks are due additional personnel who provided endless assistance in accessing the case files, most notably Lana Paiva, Third Circuit Family Court; Regina Jimenez, Fifth Circuit Family Court; and Cindy Tamashiro, First Circuit Family Court. Thanks also to the JJIS staff who provided ongoing technical support.

---

* This is an edited, reformatted and augmented version of an Department of the Attorney General of Hawaii publication dated May 2006.

EXECUTIVE SUMMARY

This report provides a statistical profile of female juvenile offenders in Hawaii. It utilizes two main datasets: (1) CY 2004 Juvenile Justice Information System data; and (2) Family Court case file information on juvenile offenders who were either on probation or incarcerated at the Hawaii Youth Correctional Facility (HYCF). The report first examines general trends in juvenile arrests and adjudications, focusing on gender and racial/ethnic differences in each category. It then analyzes gender differences in the social, psychological, family, drug use, and academic backgrounds in the case file sample. Finally, the report examines intragender differences between HYCF girls and non-HYCF girls.

What gender differences exist in juvenile arrests and adjudications?

The study data reveal that runaway and truancy were numerically and proportionally the top two charges for both boys and girls during CY 2004. However, the number of runaway arrests for girls was 47% higher than for boys, while boys had 56% more arrests for truancy. Additionally, three of the top five arrest charges for girls included status offenses: runaway, truancy, and beyond parental control. Three of the top five arrests for boys included law violations, two of which were person offenses: assault 3, theft 4, and harassment. The strongest predictor of adjudication was offense severity. However, two other predictors were also statistically significant when controlling for offense severity; juveniles who reside in Maui County and girls in general were less likely to be adjudicated.

What gender differences exist in the social, academic, drug use, mental health, and family backgrounds of juvenile offenders?

Girls' case files, versus those for boys, reveal more reports of witnessing domestic violence and experiencing physical abuse, sexual abuse, and neglect. Boys and girls differ slightly in the mental health areas. Nearly 30% of the girls, compared to 10% of the boys, have at least one prior suicide attempt recorded in their case file. Additionally, close to half of the girls' files report current or past suicidal ideation, while less than one-quarter of the boys' files contain such reports. Girls were five times more likely than boys to report self-injurious behavior (such as cutting), while boys' case files were more likely to contain reports of physical aggression. The boys' files were significantly more likely than the girls' files to document an Attention Deficit/Hyperactive Disorder (ADHD) diagnosis (23% v. 7%), while girls' files were significantly more likely to reveal a diagnosis of depression/Post-Traumatic Stress Disorder (PTSD) (28% v. 14%).

Very few variables relating to peer group and school dynamics show any significant gender differences. Based on the case file research, male and female juvenile offenders are equally likely to have failed academically and to be chronic truants. In terms of special education needs, 63% of the overall sample is certified as special education, with boys significantly more likely than girls to be so certified (67% v. 59%). There are a few statistically significant gender differences in drug use; boys have more reports of frequent marijuana use (37% v. 21% for girls), while girls are more likely to have ever tried crystal methamphetamine (or "ice," 45% v. 28% for boys). Girls are also more likely to be frequent ice users (23% v. 17% for boys), although this difference is not statistically significant.

Boys and girls in the study sample are similar in their family backgrounds:

- 1 in 10 has experienced the death of at least one parent.
- 1 in 2 has a parent who is or was involved in the criminal justice system.
- 1 in 4 has been placed in a foster care home (not *hanai* or extended family).
- 2 in 5 have no contact with their father; 1 in 5 has no contact with their mother.
- Almost 1 in 3 has a family history of suicide/mental illness.

How do HYCF girls differ from female juvenile offenders who have never been committed to the facility?

HYCF girls, compared to non-HYCF girls on probation, are significantly more likely to have histories of neglect and sexual abuse; foster care placement; relationships with older men; self-injurious behavior; frequent ice use; risky sexual behavior, including prostitution; negative peer group involvement; and academic failure. Additionally, girls with histories of neglect were over five times more likely to be committed to the HYCF than were girls without such experiences.

What is the profile of the female juvenile offender? How does it differ from the profile for boys?

Several areas distinguish female juvenile offenders in Hawaii from their male counterparts. Overall, girls differ from boys in that they are more likely to be arrested for status offenses, especially runaway; to have tried ice; to have histories of trauma, suicidal ideation, and suicide attempts; to suffer from depression/PTSD; and to engage in self-injurious behaviors. Boys, on the other hand, are more likely than girls to be arrested for law violations, particularly person crimes, and to be adjudicated for their offenses. They are also more likely than their female counterparts to engage in physically aggressive behaviors, to be certified as special education, and to be frequent marijuana users.

Policy Recommendations

This report concludes with several policy recommendations. Overall, it is recommended that "girl offender" programming should incorporate the necessary education, treatment, and other opportunities, in order to build resiliency in these girls' lives. Secondly, it is also suggested that further research on understanding boys' pathways to crime and delinquency should be conducted. Possibilities include exploring the correlation of delinquency with mental health issues (e.g., ADHD), substance abuse (specifically, frequent marijuana use), aggression, peer group dynamics, and family stressors.

INTRODUCTION

Female involvement in the juvenile justice system has emerged as a significant trend over the past three decades (Budnick and Shield-Fletcher 1998). Although the majority of juvenile arrestees have always been male, the proportion of females has been increasing. In 1975, girls accounted for 15% of all juvenile arrests. In 1990, they represented 19% and by 2004 they comprised nearly 30% (Steffensmeier 1993 FBI 2005). While overall delinquency rates have declined since the late 1990s, the decrease has not been equally shared by both boys and girls. From 1995 to 2004, boys' arrests dropped 47% for Index Offenses (including murder, forcible rape, robbery, aggravated assault, burglary, motor vehicle theft, larceny-theft, and arson) and fell 18% for Part II

Offenses (all other, less serious offenses) (FBI 2005). In comparison, girls' arrests for Index Offenses decreased 24% and fell only 5% for Part II Offense arrests (FBI 2005).

Juvenile court data also suggest a similar trend. Whereas boys represent the majority of cases handled by juvenile courts, girls now comprise one-quarter of these cases, up from 19% in 1985. In 1985, the delinquency case rate for boys was four times greater than for girls; by 2000, it was less than three times greater (OJJDP 2004). From 1985 to 2000, the overall female delinquency caseload grew by 4% per year, compared to 2% for boys (OJJDP 2004). Increases in female caseloads outpaced boys in three of the four general offenses categories: person (185% v. 88%), property (28% v. –11%), and public order (144% v. 96%) (OJJDP 2004).

Girls also comprise an increasing proportion of juveniles in custody. Between 1989 and 1998, detentions of girls increased 56%, whereas detentions of boys rose only 20% (Harms 2002). Nationally, girls comprise 18% of those in detention and 12% of those in public correctional facilities; girls in custody tend to be younger than their male counterparts and are more likely to be committed for status offenses or technical violations of probation and parole (Sickmund 2004). More than 24% of females in detention are charged with probation and parole violations, compared with only 12% of male juveniles (Poe-Yamagata and Butts 1996).

In Hawaii, juvenile delinquency has generally followed national trends, with a steady and dramatic decline in overall juvenile arrests over the last decade. From 1995 to 2004, Hawaii boys' arrests for Index Offenses plummeted 52%, while Hawaii girls' Index Offense arrests fell 55%. During this same time period, Part II Offense arrests for Hawaii boys decreased 60%, and fell 63% for their female counterparts. Additionally, runaway arrests for both boys and girls fell by 33% (Crime Prevention and Justice Assistance Division 2005). Despite this overall decline in the last decade, the proportion of girls' arrests in Hawaii is higher than it is nationally. In Hawaii, girls account for 33% of Index Offense arrests and 42% of Part II Offense arrests, both of which are up slightly from their respective proportion in 1995. While the majority of girls' arrests are for status offenses (e.g., running away, truancy, beyond parental control), girls also accounted for 31 % of juvenile arrests for "other assaults" and 39% of juvenile arrests for drug possession in 2004 (Crime Prevention and Justice Assistance Division 2005).

Because of the increasing visibility of girls in the juvenile justice system, many states have launched initiatives to better understand the relationship between female delinquency and girls' risk factors[1] (Budnick and Shield-

Fletcher 1998). Such risk factors include girls' greater likelihood to experience physical and/or sexual abuse (U.S. Department of Health and Human Services 1996); to suffer from depression and other mental disorders (Carnegie Council on Adolescent Development 1995; Timmons-Mitchell, et al. 1997); to have low self esteem and higher incidences of eating disorders, suicidal ideation and self-injury (Mullis, et al. 2004; McCabe, et al. 2002); and to experience sexual harassment and interpersonal rivalries (Acoca 1998). Other studies have shown that female juvenile offenders also have high rates of truancy and low school attachment (Sommers and Gizzi 2001; Rumberger and Lawson 1998); intergenerational patterns of criminal justice involvement (Acoca 1998); fragmented families (Acoca 1998); and residence in distressed and socially disorganized neighborhoods (Katz 2000).

Study Purpose

Given that girls account for a considerable and, by some measures, growing proportion of overall juvenile arrests, this report examines the profile of the female juvenile offender in Hawaii. The report first provides a look at general trends in juvenile arrests and adjudications, as it pays attention to gender and racial/ethnic differences. Secondly, the report examines gender differences in the social backgrounds of youth on probation versus those committed to the Hawaii Youth Correctional Facility (HYCF). Specifically, this study report addresses the following questions:

- What gender differences exist in juvenile arrests and adjudications?
- What gender differences exist in the social, academic, drug use, mental health, and family backgrounds of juvenile offenders?
- How do HYCF girls differ from female juvenile offenders who have never been committed to the facility?
- What is the profile of the female juvenile offender? How does it differ from the profile for boys?

Methods

This study first analyzed Juvenile Justice Information System (JJIS) data on all juvenile arrests made in the State of Hawaii during Calendar Year 2004.

The JJIS, housed in the State of Hawaii's Department of the Attorney General, is responsible for the development, maintenance, and implementation of a statewide database on all juvenile offenders. Agencies include county police departments, Family Courts, county prosecutors, and the HYCF. Because of the participation and coordination of these agencies, information on every juvenile who enters the justice system is available. The JJIS summarizes the information on juvenile offenders in separate tables: arrests, referrals to Family Court, and commitment to the HYCF. This report uses JJIS data to examine gender differences in arrests, demographic characteristics of arrested and adjudicated juveniles, and predictors of adjudication.

The second part of this report utilizes Family Court case files to present an analysis of probation versus HYCF youth. Juveniles in the study were either on probation or were incarcerated at the HYCF at least once during CY 2004. Every effort was made to include a variety of juvenile offenders. Low-level probationers (one or two offenses), more chronic offenders (three or more offenses, history of detainment), and juveniles at the most serious end of the spectrum (those committed to the HYCF) were all included in the study. The sample was drawn from statewide JJIS listings of juvenile probationers and three random HYCF population days. The JJIS sample reflected the proportion of juvenile probationers, by gender and by court. Accordingly, 40% of the sample were girls, 64% were from the City & County of Honolulu (Oahu), 19% were from Hawaii County, 9% were from Maui County, and 8% were from Kauai County. In the HYCF sample, girls were slightly over-sampled, representing about one-third of the analyzed case files. (Girls generally comprise 10-20% of the HYCF population). Overall, 178 probationer files and 93 HYCF files (n=271) were used. Originally, 300 files were selected for the sample, but 29 files were not used because they were either incomplete or unavailable at the time of data collection.

All study data extracted from Family Court case files (social history, academic, medical, and mental health records), and the JJIS (legal records) were kept confidential. When Child and Protective Services records were included, information covering these domains was also incorporated. See Appendix A for a complete listing of all documents examined. The following variables were explored, when available: arrest and adjudication histories; demographic characteristics (e.g., race/ethnicity, gender, age, residence); mental health diagnoses; drug use; gang involvement; peer relationships; sexual histories and orientation; school performance; histories of physical and/or sexual abuse, or neglect; family dynamics; and family histories of criminal justice involvement. See Appendix B for variable and coding definitions.

GENDER AND JUVENILE DELINQUENCY IN HAWAII

Using the 2004 JJIS data, this section of the report examines gender differences in Hawaii juvenile arrests and predictors of adjudication.

Gender Differences in Hawaii's Juvenile Arrests

Basic frequencies showing gender differences in arrests were calculated using the JJIS data. These data reveal that runaway and truancy are the top two arrest charges for both boys and girls. However, the number of girls' runaway arrests was 47% higher than the figure for boys, while boys had 56% more arrests for truancy. Boys also had twice as many arrests for assault 3 ("Assault in the Third Degree") than did girls, and almost two-thirds as many arrests for theft 4. Overall, four of the top ten arrest charges for girls included status offenses: runaway, truancy, beyond parental control, and curfew violation. Seven of the top ten arrest charges for boys included law violations, three of which were person offenses: assault 3, harassment, and terroristic threatening 2.

Table 1. Arrest Type by Gender, CY 2004

Boys	Girls
• Runaway (1,906)	• Runaway (2,808)
• Truancy (760)	• Truancy (485)
• Assault 3 (751)	• Theft 4 (441)
• Theft 4 (720)	• Assault 3 (363)
• Detrimental Drug 3 (526)	• Beyond Parental Control (298)
• Criminal Property Damage 2 (495)	• Curfew (238)
• Harassment (441)	• Harassment (172)
• Curfew Violation (393)	• Detrimental Drug 3 (154)
• Disorderly Conduct (339)	• Theft 3 (118)
• Terroristic Threatening 2 (229)	• Disorderly Conduct (115)

Predicting Adjudication

Slightly over 9% of the 17,340 juvenile arrests listed in the JJIS for 2004 ended in adjudication. The JJIS data were used to identify and examine predictors of adjudication. First, cross-tabulations between gender, race/ethnicity, and adjudication were performed, and when group differences were ascertained, Chi square (χ^2) analyses were used. An important caveat is that for the race/ethnicity variable, only the first racial/ethnic category listed in the juvenile's JJIS record was utilized. Table 2 summarizes these findings and shows that juvenile arrestees are significantly more likely to be boys than girls (62% v. 38%), and that boys are more likely to have their arrests result in adjudication (11% v. 7%). Additionally, Samoan (12%) and Hawaiian/part-Hawaiian (10%) youth were significantly more likely to have their arrests end in adjudication, while Chinese youth were least likely (6%). ("Statistical significance" is herein defined to mean that the likelihood an observed difference could occur by chance is no greater than 5%.)

Logistic regression was then performed in order to better explain these findings. Logistic regression is a predictive model that is used when the dependent or outcome variable (in this case, adjudication) is categorical with exactly two categories, e.g., adjudicated/not adjudicated. The independent variables essentially serve as predictor variables, and the logistic model estimates the relationship between them and the dependent variable. It computes the probability (odds ratio) of change in the dependent variable. In other words, once all of the independent variables are included in the statistical model, which of them have the greatest influence on the outcome variable? In this study, logistic regression was used to predict adjudication. What independent variables (circuit court location, gender, race/ethnicity, offense type) predict whether or not a juvenile will be adjudicated (dependent variable)? Once offense type and court location are controlled, does being male, Hawaiian/part-Hawaiian, or Samoan still predict whether or not a juvenile will be adjudicated?

As shown in Table 3, once offense type is controlled, race/ethnicity variables were no longer strong predictors of adjudication. The "B" coefficient indicates the strength a particular variable has in relation to the other variables in the model. With the exception of "Chinese" and "Tongan," Table 3 shows that race/ethnicity variables have among the smallest B coefficients, therefore contributing less to the predictive model. Additionally, no race/ethnicity differences were statistically significant.

Table 2. Adjudication, by Gender and Race/Ethnicity, CY 2004

Independent Variables	Adjudicated	Not Adjudicated	Total
Boys*	1,185 (11%)	9,508 (89%)	10,693 (62%)
Girls	450 (7%)	6,197 (93%)	6,647 (38%)
Hawaiian/part-Hawaiian*	521 (10%)	4,582 (90%)	5,103 (30%)
Caucasian	393 (9%)	3,994 (91%)	4,387 (25%)
Filipino	307 (9%)	3,113 (91%)	3,420 (20%)
Japanese	85 (9%)	854 (91%)	939 (6%)
Samoan*	89 (12%)	680 (88%)	769 (5%)
Black	36 (9%)	355 (91%)	391 (2%)
Chinese	15 (6%)	222 (94%)	237 (1%)
Tongan	16 (9%)	161 (91%)	177 (1%)
Micronesian	12 (8%)	140 (92%)	152 (<1%)
Korean	15 (10%)	127 (90%)	142 (<1%)
All other ethnicities	146 (9%)	1,477 (91%)	1,623 (9%)

*p< .05

Several offense-type variables served as the strongest predictors of adjudication. True to the presumed intentions of juvenile justice, the more serious the offense, the greater the likelihood of adjudication. First or second degree sexual assault arrests and robbery arrests were the strongest predictors of adjudication in the model (B=2.70 and 2.61, respectively). Juveniles arrested for these offenses were 14.84 times more likely than runaway arrestees to be adjudicated in Family Court. Robbery arrestees were 13.57 times; UCPV felony theft arrestees were 12.51 times; and family abuse and dangerous drug arrestees were each over eleven times more likely to be adjudicated than were runaway arrestees. Additionally, other types of status offense arrestees were the only other arrestees to have less chance of being adjudicated than were runaway arrestees: truancy (.26 to 1), compulsory attendance (.40 to 1), beyond parental control (.54 to 1) and injurious behavior (.81 to 1).

Gender and court location were also significant predictors of adjudication, although their overall predictive values were quite low. Regardless of offense severity, boys were 1.20 times more likely to be adjudicated than were girls, and Maui youth only had a .60 to 1 chance of being adjudicated as compared to juveniles in the City & County of Honolulu.

One limitation of these findings is that offense history (i.e., a juvenile's "rap sheet"), while potentially an extremely important predictor of adjudication, could not be readily measured in the dataset and thus was not examined in this study.

Table 3. Logistic Regression, Offense and Offender-Specific Predictors of Adjudication, CY 2004

Variables	B	Standard Error	Statistical Significance	Odds Ratio
Circuit Courts (Comparison = City & County of Honolulu)				
Maui County	-.52	.084	.000	.60 to 1
Hawaii County	.08	.08	.31	1.09 to 1
Kauai County	.08	.09	.38	1.08 to 1
Ethnicity (Comparison = Caucasian)				
Hawaiian	.04	.08	.590	1.04 to 1
Chinese	-.36	.28	.204	.70 to 1
Japanese	-.04	.13	.784	.96 to 1
Filipino	.02	.08	.78	1.02 to 1
Samoan	-.04	.14	.768	.960 to 1
Korean	.11	.29	.716	1.11 to 1
Black	-.14	.19	.453	.87 to 1
Hispanic	-.10	.55	.86	.91 to 1
Tongan	-.24	.28	.377	.78 to 1
Other ethnicity	-.23	.11	.033	.79 to 1
Arrests (Comparison = Runaway)				
Truancy	-1.33	.27	.000	.26 to 1
Compulsory attendance	-.94	.51	.07	.40 to 1
Beyond parental control	-.62	.32	.05	.54 to 1
Curfew	-.99	.37	.007	.37 to 1
Dangerous drug	2.43	.33	.000	11.33 to 1
Detrimental drug	1.07	.148	.000	2.92 to 1
Prohibitions	.72	.220	.001	2.06 to 1
Burglary	2.27	.17	.000	9.62 to 1
Theft felony	2.56	.187	.000	12.96 to 1
Theft misdemeanor	1.12	.21	.000	3.06 to 1
Theft petty misdemeanor	1.04	.12	.000	2.84 to 1
Shoplifting	.74	.28	.009	2.09 to 1
Harassment	.41	.19	.037	1.50 to 1
Disorderly conduct	.31	.25	.222	1.36 to 1
Trespassing	.86	.24	.000	2.36 to 1
Unauthorized control of a propelled vehicle	2.53	.18	.000	12.51 to 1
Unauthorized entrance of a motor vehicle	2.06	.23	.000	7.86 to 1
Criminal property damage	1.73	.13	.000	5.63 to 1

Table 3. Continued

Variables	B	Standard Error	Statistical Significance	Odds Ratio
Circuit Courts (Comparison = City & County of Honolulu)				
Driving without a license	2.13	.24	.000	8.40 to 1
Terroristic threatening	1.78	.16	.000	5.90 to 1
Injurious behavior	-.21	.46	.655	.81 to 1
Assault felony	1.99	.22	.000	7.29 to 1
Assault misdemeanor/petty misdemeanor	1.33	.12	.000	3.78 to 1
Sexual assault (first and second degree)	2.70	.27	.000	14.84 to 1
Sexual assault (third and fourth degree)	1.85	.22	.000	6.40 to 1
Robbery	2.61	.20	.000	13.57 to 1
Family abuse	2.46	.17	.000	11.75 to 1
Contempt	.89	.24	.000	2.43 to 1
Other offense	1.32	.11	.000	3.73 to 1
Gender (Comparison = Female)	.19	.06	.003	1.20 to 1
Constant	-3.21	.096	.000	.04

Dependent variable: yes/no adjudicated. N=17,340 arrests

Overall, when controlling for other variables, the strongest significant predictors of adjudication include (in order):

- Arrest for sexual assault (first or second degree)
- Arrest for robbery
- Arrest for felony theft
- Arrest for UCPV
- Arrest for family abuse
- Arrest for a dangerous drug

Predictors that significantly decrease a juvenile's chance of being adjudicated include:

- Maui residence
- Being female
- Arrests for truancy
- Arrests for curfew

- Arrests for compulsory attendance
- Arrests for injurious behavior

CASE FILE ANALYSIS

This section of the report summarizes findings from the HYCF and probationer case file analyses. Included are examinations of gender differences in offense and demographic information, abuse and sexuality variables, mental health domains, peer group and school characteristics, drug use, and family dynamics.

Age and Offense Characteristics

The age range in the sample was from 13 to 19 years old, with an average of roughly 16 years old. Girls, on average, were slightly older than boys in their age at first arrest (12.7 v. 12.0 years old), had slightly fewer overall offenses (12.4 v. 14.5), more runaway offenses (6.9 v. 4.5) more status offenses (8.2 v. 6.2), and fewer law violation offenses (1.3 v. 2.2). See Table 4.

Throughout the remainder of this report, the term "offense" is used and defined as an arrest, a referral to Family Court, or any charge/adjudication that does not have an associated preceding arrest or referral. Juveniles are referred to Family Court from different agencies (police, school, parents); sometimes they are formally arrested and other times they are not. Additionally, juveniles might have other charges added to their records during the prosecution phase of their cases. Due to the fact that they were never formally arrested for the additional charges (or, in some cases, due to data entry errors in the JJIS), these infractions do not have prior arrests or referrals "attached" to them. This report uses the term "offense" as a more expansive term that resolves these issues.

Table 4. Offense-Specific Frequencies, by Gender

Independent Variables		Boys (n=159)	Girls (n=112)
Age	Range Mean Median	13-19 years old 16.2 16.0	13-19 years old 15.8 16.0
Age at first arrest	Range Mean Median	Age 6-17 12.0 12.0	Age 9-16 12.7 13.0
Number of offenses per juvenile	Range Mean Median	1-85 offenses 14.5 10.0	1-50 offenses 12.4 9.0
Number of runaway offenses	Range Mean Median	0-50 offenses 4.5 2.0	0-31 offenses 6.9 4.5
Number of status offenses	Range Mean Median	0-57 offenses 6.2 3.0	0-34 offenses 8.2 5.0
Number of property offenses	Range Mean Median	0-14 offenses 2.5 2.0	0-12 offenses 1.6 1.0
Number of person offenses	Range Mean Median	0-14 offenses 3.4 3.0	0-12 offenses 1.4 1.0
Number of drug offenses	Range Mean Median	0-9 offenses 0.72 0.0	0-7 offenses 0.4 0.0
Number of felony offenses	Range Mean Median # of FA # of FB # of FC	0-14 offenses 2.3 2.0 27 (mean=.17) 97 (.61) 247 (1.6)	0-10 offenses 0.8 0.0 2 (mean=.02) 15 (.14) 73 (.67)
Number of misdemeanor offenses	Range Mean Median	0-22 offenses 3.1 2.0	0-10 offenses 1.8 1.0
Number of petty misdemeanor offenses	Range Mean Median	0-12 offenses 3.1 2.0	0-10 offenses 1.4 1.0

Ethnicity and Circuit Court, by Gender

Hawaiians/part-Hawaiians (43%), Caucasians (16%), Filipinos/as (14%), and Samoans (7%) comprise the majority of the case file sample. Additionally, most of the sample resides in the City & County of Honolulu.

Social, Psychological, Family, and Academic Characteristics

Table 6 shows that girls' case files more frequently report witnessing domestic violence and experiencing physical abuse, sexual abuse, and neglect. When gender differences emerged, Chi Square (χ^2) was used to determine statistical significance. Significant differences were found in experiences of domestic violence and sexual abuse: 58% of girls compared to 42% of boys were witness to domestic violence, and 38% of girls versus 8% of boys had records of sexual abuse. While not statistically significant, gender differences also emerged in neglect and physical abuse histories: 35% of girls, as opposed to 25% of boys had records of neglect, and 50% of girls compared to 41% of boys had accounts of physical abuse.

Table 5. Ethnicity and Circuit Court, by Gender

Ethnicity		Boys (n=159)	Girls (n=112)	Total (n=271)
Hawaiian/part-Hawaiian		66 *(41%)*	53 *(47%)*	119 (43%)
Caucasian		25 *(16%)*	17 *(15%)*	42 (16%)
Filipino/a		19 *(12%)*	19 *(17%)*	38 (14%)
Samoan		13 *(8%)*	7 *(6%)*	20 (7%)
Japanese		10 *(6%)*	4 *(3%)*	14 (5%)
Other Polynesian		7 *(4%)*	3 *(3%)*	10 (4%)
Hispanic		5 *(3%)*	3 *(3%)*	8 (3%)
Other Asian		4 *(3%)*	3 *(3%)*	7 (3%)
African-American		4 *(3%)*	3 *(3%)*	7 (3%)
Micronesian		6 *(4%)*	0 *(0%)*	6 (2%)
Family Court	Honolulu	99 (36%)	77 (28%)	176 (64%)
	Maui Hawaii	17 (6%)	7 (3%)	24 (9%)
	Kauai	28 (11%)	21 (8%)	49 (19%)
		15 (5%)	7 (3%)	22 (8%)

*Significant at p<.01. **Bold, *italicized numbers*** represent within gender percentages.

These findings generally parallel other research literature in that they suggest girls are more likely than boys to be victims of abuse and exposed to violence within the home. However, the current figures are also slightly higher than what previous studies on sexual abuse and domestic violence in female juvenile offender population have reported. Nationally, 35% of girls in the system have histories of sexual abuse and 40% report exposure to domestic violence (OJJDP 1996). Other studies focusing on female juvenile arrestee populations alone have shown that 22% have experienced sexual abuse (Community Action Network 2000), with girls being three times more likely to have experienced sexual abuse than have boys (U.S. Department of Health and Human Services 1996). In the current study, girls were closer to four times more likely to have reports of sexual abuse than were boys. Comparing this to the overall juvenile population in Hawaii, about 11% of all households with children have reports of domestic violence (Kids Count 2005). In this study, an average 49% of the total sample was witness to domestic violence.

Table 6. Abuse and Sexuality Variables, by Gender

Independent Variables		Boys (n=159)	Girls (n=112)	Total (n=271)
Domestic violence[*]	No	79 *(58%)*	41 *(42%)*	120 (51%)
	Yes	58 *(42%)*	57 *(58%)*	115 (49%)
Neglect	No	95 *(75%)*	56 *(65%)*	151 (71%)
	Yes	32 *(25%)*	30 *(35%)*	62 (29%)
Sexual abuse[*]	No	147 *(92%)*	70 *(62%)*	217 (80%)
	Yes	12 *(8%)*	42 *(38%)*	54 (20%)
Physical abuse	No	94 *(59%)*	56 *(50%)*	150 (55%)
	Yes	65 *(41%)*	56 *(50%)*	121 (45%)
Heterosexual[*]	No	8 *(6%)*	18 *(18%)*	26 (12%)
	Yes	120 *(94%)*	80 *(82%)*	160 (88%)
Aggressive sexual behavior[*]	No	125 *(79%)*	111 *(99%)*	236 (87%)
	Yes	34 *(21%)*	1 *(1%)*	35 (13%)
Risky sexual behavior[*]	No	154 *(97%)*	70 *(62%)*	224 (83%)
	Yes	5 *(3%)*	42 *(38%)*	47 (17%)

*Significant at p<.01. **Bold, *italicized* numbers** represent within gender percentages. When the figures do not total 271, it is due to missing values (incomplete case file information) for that variable.

Turning to sexuality variables, the majority of study boys (94%) and girls (82%) self-reported heterosexual identity. Boys' files had more reports of sexually aggressive behavior, while girls' files reported more incidences of sexually risky behaviors (see Appendix B for coding definitions). All three variables showed statistically significant differences between boys and girls in the case file sample.

Table 7 shows gender differences in psychological diagnoses, suicidal tendencies, and aggressive behaviors. In the case files, Conduct Disorder, Attention Deficit/Hyperactive Disorder (ADHD), and Depression/Post-Traumatic Stress Disorder (PTSD) were the most common diagnoses. No statistical differences exist between gender and Conduct Disorder, but boys were significantly more likely than girls to have an ADHD diagnosis (23% v. 7%), and girls were significantly more likely to have a diagnosis of depression/PTSD (28% v. 14%). This corresponds to extant literature indicating that one-half to three-fourths of juvenile offenders nationwide are estimated to suffer from a mental health disorder (Kids Count 2005).

Over 35% of the girls, compared to 12% of the boys, have at least one prior suicide attempt recorded in their case file. Additionally, over half of the girls reported current or past suicidal ideation, while only one-quarter of the boys contained such reports. These are much higher figures than exist for the general juvenile population in Hawaii. According to the Youth Risk Behavior Survey (YRBSS 2003),16-20% of juveniles in Hawaii report having previous suicidal ideation, while 10% report a prior suicide attempt.

Girls were almost six times more likely than boys to report self-injurious behavior (such as cutting), while boys were 33% more likely to have reports of physical aggression.

Very few variables relating to peer group and school dynamics showed significant gender differences. Boys and girls were equally likely to have failed academically and to be chronic truants. Over three-fourths of the total sample had failed at least one entire school semester, and over four-fifths had current or prior records of chronic truancy. Both boys and girls were likely to be part of negative peer groups (slightly higher for girls), and the extent of gang involvement, overall, was low.

In terms of special education needs, 63% of the total sample were certified as special education, with boys significantly more likely than girls to be so certified (67% v. 59%). Relationships with older men rarely showed up in boys' files, while it was commonly reported in the girls' files; girls were over six times more likely to have reports of a peer group that contained older men (5+ years older).

Table 7. Mental Health Variables, by Gender

Independent Variables		Boys (n=159)	Girls (n=112)	Total (n=271)
Conduct Disorder	No	128 *(81%)*	98 *(87%)*	226 (83%)
	Yes	31 *(19%)*	14 *(13%)*	45(17%)
ADHD[*]	No	122 *(77%)*	104 *(93%)*	226 (83%)
	Yes	37 *(23%)*	8 *(7%)*	45 (17%)
Depression/PTSD[*]	No	137 *(86%)*	81 *(72%)*	218 (80%)
	Yes	22 *(14%)*	31 *(28%)*	53 (20%)
Suicidal Ideation (past or present)[*]	No	112 *(75%)*	49 *(47%)*	161 (64%)
	Yes	37 *(25%)*	55 *(53%)*	92 (36%)
Previous suicide attempts[*]	No	123 (88%)	61 *(65%)*	184 (79%)
	Yes	16 *(12%)*	33 *(35%)*	49 (21 %)
Self-injurious behaviors[*]	No	150 (95%)	81 *(72%)*	231 (85%)
	Yes	9 *(5%)*	31 *(28%)*	40 (15%)
History of physically assaultive behavior[*]	No	23 *(14%)*	41 *(36%)*	64 (24%)
	Yes	136 *(86%)*	71 *(64%)*	207 (76%)

*Significant at p<.01. **Bold, *italicized* numbers** represent within gender percentages. When the figures do not total 271, it is due to missing values (incomplete case file information) for that variable.

Table 8. Peer Group and School Variables, by Gender

Independent Variables		Boys (n=159)	Girls (n=112)	Total (n=271)
Negative peer group	No	24 *(39%)*	14 *(14%)*	38(17%)
	Yes	97 *(80%)*	84 *(86%)*	181(83%)
Gang involvement	No	114 *(85%)*	93 *(92%)*	207 (86%)
	Yes	24 *(17%)*	9 *(8%)*	33 (13%)
Academic failure	No	35 *(23%)*	26 *(24%)*	61 (23%)
	Yes	120 *(77%)*	84 *(76%)*	204 (77%)
Chronic truancy	No	29 *(28%)*	19 *(22%)*	48 (19%)
	Yes	114 *(80%)*	87 *(82%)*	201 (81%)
Special education[*]	No	53 *(33%)*	46 *(41%)*	99 (37%)
	Yes	106 *(67%)*	66 *(59%)*	172 (63%)
Older male relationships[*]	No	149 *(94%)*	68 *(61%)*	217 (80%)
	Yes	10 *(6%)*	44 *(39%)*	54 (20%)

*Significant at p<.01. **Bold, *italicized* numbers** represent within gender percentages. When the figures do not total 271, it is due to missing values (incomplete case file information) for that variable.

Three-fourths of the total sample reported some form of drug use and 77% reported some form of alcohol use in their lifetimes. Two-fifths of the sample had reports of frequent drug use, with slightly more boys (43%) than girls (36%) reporting frequent use. Boys had significantly more reports of frequent marijuana use (37% of the sample), while girls had significantly more reports of frequent ice use (23%). Girls were two-thirds more likely than boys to have used ice at least once in their lifetimes. In comparison, 47% of statewide youth report trying marijuana at least once in their lifetimes, while only 8% report using ice at least once (YRBS, 2003).

Table 9. Drug Use, by Gender

Independent Variables		Boys (n=159)	Girls (n=112)	Total (n=271)
Alcohol use ever	No	36 *(26%)*	25 *(22%)*	61 (22%)
	Yes	118 *(77%)*	87 *(78%)*	205 (77%)
Frequent alcohol use	No	148 *(93%)*	106 *(95%)*	254 (94%)
	Yes	11 *(7%)*	6 *(5%)*	17 (16%)
Marijuana use ever	No	37 *(24%)*	29 *(27%)*	66 (25%)
	Yes	121 *(76%)*	82 *(73%)*	203 (75%)
Frequent marijuana use[*]	No	100 *(63%)*	88 *(79%)*	188 (69%)
	Yes	59 *(37%)*	24 *(21%)*	83 (31 %)
Ice use ever[*]	No	114 *(72%)*	62 *(55%)*	176 (64%)
	Yes	45 *(28%)*	50 *(45%)*	95 (36%)
Frequent ice user	No	132 *(83%)*	86 *(77%)*	218 (81%)
	Yes	27 *(17%)*	26 *(23%)*	53 (19%)
Other drugs used	No	120 *(85%)*	79 *(80%)*	199 (83%)
	Yes	21 *(15%)*	20 *(20%)*	41 (17%)

*Significant at p<.01. **Bold, *italicized* numbers** represent within gender percentages. When the figures do not total 271, it is due to missing values (incomplete case file information) for that variable.

Additionally, recent studies of youth who frequently use methamphetamine have found these juveniles to be more likely to have driven drunk, been in a fight within the last month, and attempted suicide (Dodge Data Systems 2005).

No statistically significant gender differences were found in the family variables in this study. Boys and girls were about as likely to have an absent father, an absent mother, and some form of parental involvement in their lives. About 75% of the sample lives in single-parent households, which is three times higher than the rate found in Hawaii's overall juvenile population (Kids

Count 2005). Boys and girls in the study were about as likely to experience the death of a parent or a significant other (such as grandparents, siblings, boy/girlfriends, best friends, etc.). Over half of the sample has at least one parent involved as an offender in the criminal justice system, and 65% have parents who have abused drugs or alcohol. Nearly one-third (31%) has a history of mental illness within their families.

Table 10. Family Variables, by Gender

Independent Variables		Boys (n=159)	Girls (n=112)	Total (n=271)
Absent father	No	92 *(58%)*	69 *(62%)*	161 (59%)
	Yes	67 *(42%)*	43 *(38%)*	110 (41%)
Absent mother	No	129 *(81%)*	91 *(81%)*	220 (81%)
	Yes	30 *(19%)*	21 *(19%)*	51 (19%)
Parental involvement	No	29 *(18%)*	18 *(16%)*	47 (18%)
	Yes	130 *(82%)*	94 *(84%)*	224 (82%)
History of foster care placements (not *hanai*, or extended, family)	No	121 *(76%)*	75 *(67%)*	196 (72%)
	Yes	38 *(24%)*	37 *(33%)*	75 (28%)
Death of a parent	No	141 *(88%)*	99 *(88%)*	240 (88%)
	Yes	18 *(12%)*	13 *(12%)*	31 (12%)
Death of a significant other (besides parent)	No	138 *(88%)*	92 *(84%)*	230 (86%)
	Yes	19 *(12%)*	17 *(16%)*	36 (14%)
Parents abuse drugs or alcohol	No	51 *(35%)*	37 *(35%)*	88 (35%)
	Yes	96 *(65%)*	68 *(65%)*	164 (65%)
Parents in criminal justice system	No	77 *(51%)*	47 *(43%)*	124 (48%)
	Yes	74 *(49%)*	62 *(57%)*	36 (52%)
History of mental disease in family	No	66 *(73%)*	35 *(62%)*	101 (69%)
	Yes	24 *(27%)*	22 *(38%)*	46 (31%)

*Significant at p<.01. **Bold, *italicized* numbers** represent within gender percentages. When the figures do not total 271, it is due to missing values (incomplete case file information) for that variable.

For both boys and girls:

- 1 in 10 has experienced the death of at least one parent.
- 1 in 2 has had a parent involved in the criminal justice system.
- 1 in 4 has been placed in a foster care home (not *hanai*, or extended, family).

- 41% has no contact with their father; 19% has no contact with their mother.
- Almost 1 in 3 has a family history of suicide/mental illness.

Predicting Runaway Arrests

Since runaway arrests are a dominant feature of female juvenile offending, this study performed an Ordinary Least Squares (OLS) regression, or multiple regression, as a method of predicting this offense. Controlling for other offense categories (since runaway arrests often correlate with property and drug offending) and several risk factors, the model examines the net effect that gender has on runaway arrests.

The "B" coefficients in the model indicate the effect of each independent variable, that is, how much the value of the dependent variable (the number of runaway arrests) increases or decreases, once that independent variable is included in the model. The standardized coefficients (beta) give the overall explanatory power of each independent variable; the closer to 1.00 the beta value is, the more predictive that particular independent variable becomes. For example, juveniles residing in the City & County of Honolulu average 3.02 more runaway arrests than do those who reside in other counties. That variable, Honolulu residence, is the fourth most explanatory predictor in the model (beta=.18) and is also statistically significant at p<.01 (i.e., the difference is no more than 1% likely due to chance). Similarly, for every property arrest a juvenile has, his/her runaway arrest tally increases by an average of 1.09, with that variable having the most explanatory power (.35).

Gender was the second most explanatory predictor, with a beta of .20. Girls had 3.03 more runaway arrests than did boys, regardless of other offending or risk factors.

Frequent drug use and suicidal ideation also were significant predictors of runaway arrests. Frequent drug users (beta=.23) had 3.62 more arrests for runaways than did non-frequent users, and juveniles reporting suicidal ideation (beta=.14) had 2.18 more arrests.

Overall, the following variables are the strongest predictors of runaway arrests:

- Being female
- City & County of Honolulu residence
- Multiple property arrests

- Frequent drug use
- Suicidal ideation

Table 11. OLS Regression, Predictors of Runaway Arrests

Independent Variables	Unstandardized Coefficients		Standardized Coefficients
	B	Standard Error	Beta
Female[**]	3.03	1.02	.20
City & County of Honolulu residence[**]	3.02	.99	.18
Number of property arrests[**]	1.09	.19	.35
Number of violent arrests	-.01	.17	-.00
Number of drug arrests	.49	.36	.08
Frequent drug user[**]	3.62	.90	.23
Domestic violence	-.95	.99	-.06
Abuse and neglect	1.43	.95	.09
Special education	.89	.98	.06
Suicidal ideation[*]	2.18	1.02	.14
Parent previous criminal history	1.11	.96	.07

Dependent Variable: number of runaway arrests, Adj R^2 .318, *p< .05, **p< .01

HYCF Girls and Non-HYCF Girls

This report next examines differences between chronic (HYCF commitment, n=27) and "not as chronic" (no HYCF commitment, n=85) female juvenile offenders. Cross-tabulations were completed on all aforementioned variables in this study. When differences emerged, Chi Square (χ^2) was used to determine statistical significance.

HYCF girls had an average of 25.0 arrests, and two-thirds of them were committed to HYCF for probation violations. Over three-fourths of the HYCF girls had at least one parent involved as an offender in the criminal justice system. Conversely, non-HYCF girls had an average of 7.78 arrests, and less than one-half of them had one or more parents in the criminal justice system. Examining other differences between these two groups, HYCF girls were significantly more likely to have the following characteristics:

- Histories of neglect and sexual abuse
- Histories of foster care placement (not *hanai*, or extended, family)

- Relationships with older men
- Self-injurious behavior
- Frequent ice use
- Risky sexual behavior, including prostitution
- Negative peer group
- Academic failure (all of the HYCF girls in the sample failed academically)

This study also used logistic regressions to examine intra-gender predictors of HYCF com-mitment. Controlling for offense type (status, person, property, drug), separate regressions individually underscoring the above variables were performed. Table 12 presents the summary of the variables' odds ratios. Two variables—neglect and frequent ice use—were significant predictors of HYCF commitment. Girls with histories of neglect were, on average, 5.33 times more likely to be committed to HYCF than were girls without neglect histories. Girls with frequent ice use were 5.91 times more likely to be committed to HYCF than were girls without frequent ice use.

SUMMARY: A PROFILE OF THE FEMALE JUVENILE OFFENDER

The findings reported in this study support the popular contention in existing research literature that girls (1) have become a more sizable part of the juvenile offender population; and (2) in terms of delinquency, female juvenile offenders differ from their male counterparts in certain characteristics and experiences. In this study, those experiences predominantly included prior victimization and crystal methamphetamine abuse. Lastly, this study demonstrated that some gender similarities between male and female juvenile offenders are also apparent, chiefly in the school and family domains.

In comparison to their male counterparts, the female juvenile offender in Hawaii is more likely to:

- Have tried ice
- Have a history of victimization
- Have suicidal ideation and previous suicide attempts
- Experience depression/PTSD
- Engage in self-injurious behaviors

- Be arrested for status offenses, especially runaway

Table 12. Predictors of HYCF Commitment for Female Juvenile Offenders

Variables	Odds Ratio
Neglect*	5.33 to 1
Sexual abuse	2.80 to 1
Foster care placement	2.41 to 1
Relationships with older men	1.58 to 1
Self injury	1.91 to 1
Frequent ice use*	5.91 to 1
Risky sexual behavior	3.08 to 1
Negative peer group	1.80 to 1
Academic failure	1.80 to 1

* $p < .05$

Boys, on the other hand, are more likely than girls to be arrested for law violations, particularly person crimes, and to be adjudicated for their offenses. They are also more likely to engage in physically assaultive behaviors, to be certified as in need of special education, and to be frequent marijuana users.

Male and female juvenile offenders are equally likely to have failed academically and/or be chronic truants, to have experienced the death of at least one parent, to have parents who use drugs or alcohol, and to have parents who have been through the criminal justice system. They are also equally likely to have used marijuana or alcohol at least once in their lifetime.

Key differences exist between HYCF girls and non-HYCF girls. HYCF girls have significantly more histories of neglect, sexual abuse, and foster care placement than do nonHYCF girls. The pathway to chronic offending (HYCF commitment) for girls includes parents involved in the criminal justice system, relationships with older men that are almost invariably tied to other problems, more offending (running away), negative peer groups, more drug use, and more self-injurious behaviors.

POLICY RECOMMENDATIONS

The findings of this report suggest that there is a need to understand and address the differences between male and female juvenile offenders, as well as the differences within the female juvenile offender population. The following programming recommendations are offered for girls[2]:

(1) Recognize the variation in female juvenile offenders' lives and create individualized plans that build resiliency for them;

(2) Provide a safe forum for girls to openly discuss their experiences with abuse and victimization and personal safety issues;

(3) Develop opportunities for girls to develop trusting and healthy relationships within their peer group and with age-appropriate boyfriends;

(4) Provide a safe forum to address family dynamics and problems that might contribute to delinquency pathways;

(5) Include education on female health, along with opportunities for girls to understand and define healthy sexuality and to develop positive body images;

(6) Offer appropriate treatment for depression/PTSD, suicidal ideation and attempts, and self-injurious behaviors;

(7) Provide education on and treatment for substance abuse, especially ice dependence;

(8) Engage mentors who enjoy working with girls, who share common experiences with female juvenile offenders, and who have led successful lives (perhaps despite a delinquent past);

(9) Create programs that assist girls in living independently and in building career options;

(10) Provide opportunities for girls to make changes that positively affect themselves and their communities.

In addition to these recommendations, it is also suggested that further research on understanding boys' pathways to crime and delinquency be similarly explored. Specific research recommendations include exploring the correlation between delinquency and mental health issues (Conduct Disorder, ADHD), substance abuse (specifically, frequent marijuana use), aggression, peer group dynamics, and family stressors.

REFERENCES

Acoca, L. (1998). "Outside/Inside: The Violation of American Girls at Home, in the Streets, and in the System." *Crime and Delinquency, 44,* 561-590.

Budnick, K. & Shield-Fletcher, E. (1998). *"What About Girls?"* Washington, DC: Washington, DC: U.S. Department of Justice.

Carnegie Council on Adolescent Development, (1995). *Great Transitions: Preparing A doles- cents for a New Century.* New York: Carnegie Corporation of New York.

Community Action Network. (2000). *Public Safety: Predictors of Crime.* Austin, TX: Community Action Network.

Crime Prevention and Justice Assistance Division. (2005). *Crime in Hawaii, 2004.* State of Hawaii: Department of the Attorney General.

Dodge Data Systems. (2005). *Risk Behaviors of Montana Youth: Methamphetamine Users versus non-Users.* Helena, Montana: Office of Public Instruction.

Federal Bureau of Investigation. (2005). *Uniform Crime Reports, 2004.* Washington, DC: US Department of Justice.

Harms, P. (2002). *Detention in Delinquency Cases, 1989-1998 (OJJDP Fact Sheet, No.1).* Washington, DC: US Department of Justice.

Katz, R. S. (2000). "Explaining Girls' and Women's Crime and Desistance in the Context of Their Victimization Experiences." *Violence Against Women, 6,* 633-660.

Kids Count. (2005). *2005 Kids Count Databook.* Baltimore, MD: Anne Casey Foundation.

McCabe, K. M., Lansing, A. E., Garland, A. & Hough, R. (2002). "Gender Differences in Psychopathology, Functional Impairment, and Familial Risk Factors Among Adjudicated Delinquents." *Journal of the American Academy of Child and Adolescent Psychiatry, 47,* 860- 868.

Mullis, R. L., Cornille, T., Mullis, A. & Huber, J. (2004). "Female Juvenile Offending: A Review of Characteristics and Contents." *Journal of Child and Family Studies, 13,* 205-218.

Office of Juvenile Justice and Delinquency Prevention. (2004). *Juvenile Court Statistics 2000.* Washington, DC: US Department of Justice.

Office of Juvenile Justice and Delinquency Prevention. (1998). *Juvenile Female Offenders: A Status of the States Report.* Washington, DC: U.S. Department of Justice.

Office of Juvenile Justice and Delinquency Prevention. (1996). *Female Offenders in the Juvenile Justice System*. Washington, DC: U.S. Department of Justice.

Poe-Yamagata, E. & Butts, J. A. (1996). *Female Offenders in the Juvenile Justice System: Statistics Summary*. Office of Juvenile Justice and Delinquency Prevention, Washington, DC.

Rumberger, R. W. & Lawson, K. A. (1998). "Student Mobility and Increased Risk of High School Dropout." *American Journal of Education, 107*, 1-35.

Sickmund, M. (2004). *Juveniles in Corrections*. Office of Juvenile Justice and Delinquency Prevention, Washington, DC.

Somers, C. L. & Gizzi, T. L. (2001). "Predicting Adolescents' Risky Behaviors: The Influence of Future Orientation, School Involvement, and School Attachment." *Adolescent and Family Health, 2*, 3-11.

Steffensmeier, D. (1993). "National Trends in Female Arrests, 1960-1990: Assessment and Recommendations for Research." *Journal of Quantitative Criminology, 9(4)*, 415.

Timmons-Mitchell, J, Brown, C., Schulz, C., Webster, S. E., Underwood, L. A. & Semple, W. E. (1997). "Comparing the Mental Health Needs of Female and Male Incarcerated Juvenile Delinquents." *Behavioral Science Law, 15*, 195-202.

U.S. Department of Health and Human Services. 1996. *National Incidences of Child Abuse and Neglect*. Washington, DC: U.S. Department of Health and Human Services.

Wasserman, Gail, A., Kate Keenan, Richard, E. Tremblay, John, D. Coie, Todd I. Herrenkohl, Rolf Loeber, & David Petechuk. (2003). *Risk and Protective Factors of Child Delinquency*. Washington, DC: Office of Juvenile Justice and Delinquency Prevention.

Youth Risk Behavior Surveillance System. (2003). *Healthy Youth*. Centers for Disease Control and Prevention. U.S. Department of Health and Human Services. [available online at www.cdc.gov/HealthyYouth]

APPENDIX A. DOCUMENTS ANALYZED

Referral History/ Index Report—the legal record of every youth

Family Court Officer Report—the explanation of circumstances surrounding the delinquent act as offered by the Court

Honolulu Police Department Criminal Investigation Unit's summary reports (if applicable) Detention/ HYCF intake forms and progress reports

Probation officers' social information/histories and progress reports

All Psychologist and/or Psychiatrist reports/diagnostic assessments

All substance abuse counselors' assessments

(*When more than one psychological assessment was available, the most current one was utilized*)

Urinalysis drug tests (UAs)

DOE individual education plans (IEPs) and progress reports

Teacher comments/ guidance counselor comments/school attendance cards

Child and Protective Services assessments and reports (if applicable)

Guardian Ad litem reports (if applicable)

Juvenile's personal journals, other writings, letters, testimonies, apologies

APPENDIX B: CODING DEFINITIONS

Absent father	No contact with father.
Absent mother	No contact with mother.
ADHD	Most current psychological assessment with Axis I first diagnosis of ADHD.
Aggressive sexual behavior	Arrests for sexual assault; psychological assessment confirming sexually offensive behaviors; reports by parent, victim, staff, or PO of sexual assault/ attempted assault by juvenile.
Alcohol use ever	Self-reports, treatment providers' account, parents' reports of any alcohol use.
Chronic truancy	As evidenced by attendance cards/ arrests/ DOE referrals to Family Court.
Conduct Disorder	Most current psychological assessment with Axis I first diagnosis of Conduct Disorder.
Death of a parent	(Self-explanatory.)
Death of a significant other	Besides parent, death of a close family member (such as grandparent), role model, friend, or boy/girlfriend.
Depression/PTSD	Most current psychological assessment with Axis I first diagnosis of Depression NOS, dysthymia, PTSD, or bereavement.
Domestic violence	Reports of domestic violence/abuse of family in PO's social information/ history, psych reports, parents' CJIS records, and/or CPS files.
Frequent alcohol use	Self-reports, treatment providers' account, parents' reports of alcohol intoxication, exceeding three times a week. Or official diagnosis of alcohol dependence.
Frequent ice use	Self-reports, treatment providers' account, parents' reports of ice use, exceeding three times a week; official diagnosis of methamphetamine dependence; positive UAs.
Frequent marijuana user	Self-reports, treatment providers' account, parents' reports of marijuana intoxication, exceeding three times a week; official diagnosis of cannabis de-pendence; numerous positive UAs.
Gang involvement	Police reports, self-reports, PO or other staff reports of gang membership, such as gang tattoos.
Heterosexual	Self-report in file.

Table (Continued)

History of foster care placements	CPS reports, PO reports of foster care placements, outside extended or hanai family, therapeutic group homes included.
History of mental illness in the family	Immediate family member committed suicide/ known mental health treatment of mental disorders.
History of physical aggression	Self-reports; victims' reports; arrest reports of juvenile causing physical injury to another party.
Ice use ever	Self-reports, treatment providers' account, parents' reports of any ice use.
Marijuana use ever	Self-reports, treatment providers' account, parents' reports of any use of marijuana.
Negative peer group	PO or self-reports of friends/siblings who are known to Family or Adult Court; self reports by juveniles that friends/siblings engage in delinquent behaviors; parental disapproval of friends b/c of delinquent behaviors.
Neglect	Reports of juvenile being malnourished or undernourished, abandoned, unsupervised for lengthy periods of time, unkempt, or claims of "neglect" in psych, PO, or CPS reports.
Older male relationships	Parental, PO, or self reports of male friends more than 5 years the juvenile senior. PO, parental, or self reports of boyfriends or pimps more than 5 years juvenile's senior.
Parental involvement	Juvenile has contact with at least one parent (biological, hanai, or adoptive) who is involved in his/her well-being, as evidenced in PO reports, psychological assessments, and/or school records.
Parents abuse drugs or alcohol	Parents' self-reports; CJIS reports of parents' intoxication; CPS or PO reports of parental drug/alcohol use; juvenile's self reports.
Parents in criminal justice system	Parents have CJIS record for felony arrests, as evidenced by printouts in case files; parents are/were on probation or parole; parents are/were in prison.
Physical abuse	Juvenile self-reports of physical abuse; parents' report of physical abuse; criminal and/or CPS confirmation of physical abuse.
Previous suicide attempts	Self-reports; hospitalization/treatment for suicide attempt; Staff, parents' or peers' reports of attempts.

Table (Continued)

Risky sexual behavior	Self-reports of unprotected sex with multiple partners; juvenile has been pregnant/made someone pregnant; has an STD; self reports of, parents' reports of, or arrests for prostitution.
Self injurious behaviors	Self-reports, physical scars, or previous treatment/hospitalization for cutting, burning, or other physically self-injurious behaviors.
Sexual abuse	Self-reports of sexual abuse or assault; parents' report of sexual abuse; criminal and/or CPS confirmation of sexual abuse or sexual assault.
Special education	In special education curriculum for any qualifying reason (certified).
Suicidal ideation, past or present	Self-reports; hospitalization/treatment for suicidal ideation; PO, parents' or peers' reports.

End Notes

[1] Risk factors are characteristics and experiences that may influence youth to engage in delinquent acts, such as drug use, negative peers, school failure, etc. (Wasserman, et al. 2003).

[2] See Female Delinquents Committed to the Illinois Department of Corrections: A Profile at *www.icjia.state.il.us/public/pdf/ResearchReports/FemaleDel_IDOC.pdf.* for similar findings and recommendations.

In: Not So Nice: Girls' Delinquency Issues   ISBN: 978-1-60876-268-2
Editor: Adam P. Mawer   © 2010 Nova Science Publishers, Inc.

Chapter 3

JUVENILE JUSTICE: TECHNICAL ASSISTANCE AND BETTER DEFINED EVALUATION PLANS WILL HELP TO IMPROVE GIRLS' DELINQUENCY PROGRAMS*

Eileen Regen Larence

July 24, 2009
The Honorable Robert C. Scott
Chairman
Subcommittee on Crime, Terrorism, and Homeland Security
Committee on the Judiciary
House of Representatives

Subject: *Juvenile Justice: Technical Assistance and Better Defined Evaluation Plans Will Help to Improve Girls' Delinquency Programs*

Dear Mr. Chairman:

---

* This is an edited, reformatted and augmented version of a U. S. Government Accountability Office publication dated July 2009.

Girls' delinquency has attracted the attention of federal, state, and local policymakers for more than a decade as girls have increasingly become involved in the juvenile justice system. For example, from 1995 through 2005, delinquency caseloads for girls in juvenile justice courts nationwide increased 15 percent while boys' caseloads decreased by 12 percent. Also, from 1995 through 2005, the number of girls' cases nationwide involving detention increased 49 percent compared to a 7 percent increase for boys.[1] More recently, in 2007, 29 percent of juvenile arrests—about 641,000 arrests—involved girls, who accounted for 17 percent of juvenile violent crime arrests and 35 percent of juvenile property crime arrests.[2] Further, in a 2007 survey of states conducted by the Federal Advisory Committee on Juvenile Justice, 22 states listed girls' delinquency as an issue affecting their states' juvenile justice systems.[3] State justice officials responding to the survey noted that juvenile female offenses have increased sharply and also noted that juvenile female offenders generally had more serious and wide-ranging service needs than juvenile male offenders, including treatment for substance abuse and mental health conditions.

The Office of Juvenile Justice and Delinquency Prevention (OJJDP) is the Department of Justice (DOJ) office charged with providing national leadership, coordination, and resources to prevent and respond to juvenile delinquency and victimization. OJJDP supports states and communities in their efforts to develop and implement effective programs to, among other things, prevent delinquency and intervene after a juvenile has offended. For example, from fiscal years 2007 through 2009, Congress provided OJJDP almost $1.1 billion for grants to states, localities, and organizations for a variety of juvenile justice programs. In support of this mission, the office also funds research and program evaluations related to a variety of juvenile justice issues, including girls' delinquency.

As programs have been developed at the state and local levels in recent years that specifically target preventing girls' delinquency or intervening after girls have become involved in the juvenile justice system, it is important that agencies providing grants and practitioners operating the programs have information about which of these programs are effective. In this way, agencies can help to ensure that limited federal, state, and local funds are well spent. In general, effectiveness is determined through program evaluations, which are systematic studies conducted to assess how well a program is working—that is, whether a program produced its intended effects. To help ensure that grant funds are being used effectively, you asked us to review OJJDP's efforts related to studying and promoting effective girls' delinquency programs. This report addresses the following questions:

1. What efforts, if any, has OJJDP made to assess the effectiveness of girls' delinquency programs?
2. To what extent are OJJDP's efforts to assess girls' delinquency programs consistent with generally accepted social science standards and the internal control standard to communicate with external stakeholders?
3. What are the findings from OJJDP's efforts to assess the effectiveness of girls' delinquency programs, and how, if at all, does OJJDP plan to address the findings from these efforts?

To identify OJJDP's efforts to assess the effectiveness of girls' delinquency programs, we analyzed relevant laws related to the office's role in supporting research and evaluations on delinquency programs. We also analyzed OJJDP budget data for fiscal years 2007 through 2009. We chose these years because they provide the most recent overview of the funding the office has had available to support its evaluation activities. We examined reports from research organizations and academic journal articles on girls' delinquency issues. In our review, we focused on OJJDP's efforts related to programs that are specifically designed for girls, not programs designed for both girls and boys. To identify OJJDP's efforts, we reviewed a list of its grants to fund studies of girls' delinquency programs from 1998 to 2008. We chose this time frame, the past 10 years from the start of our work, because it provided us with an overview of OJJDP's efforts related to assessing girls' delinquency programs. We also analyzed documentation about OJJDP's establishment of a study group on girls' delinquency issues, including the program announcement and cooperative agreement.[4] We interviewed OJJDP officials, including the research coordinator who managed the study group project, about the office's role in overseeing the group's research. We also interviewed the current and former principal investigators of the study group project regarding the formation of the group, its activities, and its methodologies. To gather information on OJJDP's efforts, we conducted interviews with 18 girls' delinquency subject matter experts, that is, researchers and practitioners. We selected these experts based on their knowledge and experience with girls' delinquency issues, which we determined through our review of the literature and from suggestions of experts to interview from study group members and OJJDP.[5] These 18 experts included 11 of the 15 study group members and 7 experts who were not members of the group.[6] While their comments cannot be generalized to all girls' delinquency experts, we nonetheless believe that their views gave us useful insights on issues related to girls' delinquency and OJJDP's efforts to assess girls' programs.

To determine the extent to which OJJDP's efforts to assess girls' delinquency programs were consistent with generally accepted social science standards, we reviewed the criteria the study group used to assess studies of girls' delinquency programs and whether the group's application of those criteria was consistent with standards for evaluation research.[7] To determine the extent to which these OJJDP efforts were consistent with the internal control standard to communicate with external stakeholders, we compared the office's efforts with criteria in *Standards for Internal Control in the Federal Government*, specifically that agency management should ensure that there are adequate means of obtaining information from and communicating with external stakeholders who may have a significant impact on the agency achieving its goals.[8] We reviewed documentation about the composition of the study group and the criteria used to select the group members, such as their relevant fields of expertise, knowledge, and experience with girls' issues. We also examined the study group's external communications efforts, including its Web site, findings bulletins, conference presentations, academic journal articles, and published book. In addition, we interviewed OJJDP officials about these dissemination efforts, as well as 18 girls' delinquency experts regarding their views on the composition of the study group.

To determine the findings from OJJDP's efforts to assess the effectiveness of girls' delinquency programs, and to assess how, if at all, OJJDP plans to address these findings, we analyzed documentation such as published bulletins and conference presentations about the study group's findings and recommendations related to program effectiveness. We also interviewed OJJDP officials knowledgeable about the office's planning efforts and the current and former study group principal investigators regarding the group's findings and recommendations. We compared OJJDP's stated plans with criteria in standard practices for program management.[9]

We conducted this performance audit from July 2008 through July 2009 in accordance with generally accepted government auditing standards. Those standards require that we plan and perform the audit to obtain sufficient, appropriate evidence to provide a reasonable basis for our findings and conclusions based on our audit objectives. We believe that the evidence obtained provides a reasonable basis for our findings and conclusions based on our audit objectives.

RESULTS IN BRIEF

To assess the effectiveness of girls' delinquency programs, OJJDP established the Girls Study Group (Study Group). With an overall goal of developing research that communities need to make sound decisions about how best to prevent and reduce girls' delinquency, the Study Group was established in 2004 under a $2.6 million multiyear cooperative agreement with a research institute. OJJDP's objectives for the group, among others, included identifying effective or promising programs, program elements, and implementation principles (i.e., guidelines for developing programs) and developing program models to help inform communities of what works in preventing or reducing girls' delinquency; identifying gaps in girls' delinquency research and developing recommendations for future research; and disseminating findings to the girls' delinquency field about effective or promising programs. To meet OJJDP's objectives, among other things, the Study Group identified studies of delinquency programs that specifically targeted girls. The group then assessed the methodological quality of the studies using a set of criteria developed by DOJ's Office of Justice Programs (OJP) called What Works to determine whether the studies provided credible evidence that the programs were effective at preventing or responding to girls' delinquency.[10]

OJJDP's effort to assess girls' delinquency programs through the use of a study group and the group's methods for assessing studies were consistent with generally accepted social science research practices and standards, and OJJDP's efforts to involve practitioners in Study Group activities and disseminate findings were also consistent with the internal control standard to communicate with external stakeholders.[11]

- According to OJJDP officials—including the research coordinator— they formed the Study Group rather than funding individual studies of programs because study groups provide a cost-effective method of gaining an overview of the available research in an issue area. As part of its work, the group collected, reviewed, and analyzed the methodological quality of research on girls' delinquency programs.

The use of such a group, including its review, is an acceptable approach for systematically identifying and reviewing research conducted in a field of study. This review helped consolidate the research and provide information to OJJDP for determining evaluation priorities. Further, we reviewed the criteria the group used to assess the studies and found that they adhere to generally accepted social science standards for evaluation research. We also generally concurred with the group's assessments of the programs based on these criteria. According to the group's former principal investigator, the Study Group decided to use the What Works criteria to ensure that its assessment of program effectiveness would be based on highly rigorous evaluation standards, thus eliminating the potential that a program that may do harm would be endorsed by the group. However, 8 of the 18 experts we interviewed said that the criteria created an unrealistically high standard, which caused the group to overlook potentially promising programs. OJJDP officials stated that despite such concerns, they approved the group's use of the criteria because of the methodological rigor of the framework and their goal for the group to identify effective programs.

- In accordance with the internal control standard to communicate with external stakeholders, OJJDP sought to ensure a range of stakeholder perspectives related to girls' delinquency by requiring that Study Group members possess knowledge and experience with girls' delinquency and demonstrate expertise in relevant social science disciplines. The initial Study Group, which was convened by the research institute and approved by OJJDP, included 12 academic researchers and 1 practitioner, a member with experience implementing girls' delinquency programs. Eleven of the 18 experts we interviewed stated that this composition was imbalanced in favor of academic researchers, six of whom said that the composition led the group to focus its efforts on researching theories of girls' delinquency rather than gathering and disseminating actionable information for practitioners.[12] According to OJJDP officials, they acted to address this issue by adding a second practitioner as a member and involving two other practitioners in study group activities. OJJDP officials stated that they plan to more fully involve practitioners from the beginning when they organize study groups in the future and to include practitioners in the remaining activities of the Study Group, such as presenting findings at a national conference.

Also, in accordance with the internal control standard, OJJDP and the Study Group have disseminated findings to the research community, practitioners in the girls' delinquency field, and the public through conference presentations, Web site postings, and published bulletins and plan to report on all of the group's activities by spring 2010.

To address the Study Group findings that few girls' delinquency programs had been studied and that the available studies lacked conclusive evidence of program effectiveness, OJJDP plans to provide technical assistance to help programs be better prepared for evaluation; however, more fully developing plans for supporting evaluations could help OJJDP address its girls' delinquency goals. The Study Group found that the majority of the girls' delinquency programs it identified—44 of the 61—had not been studied by researchers. For the 17 programs that had been studied, the Study Group reported that none of the studies provided conclusive evidence with which to determine whether the programs were effective at preventing or reducing girls' delinquency. For example, according to the Study Group, 11 of the 17 studies lacked evidence of program effectiveness because, for instance, the studies involved research designs that could not demonstrate whether any positive outcomes, such as reduced delinquency, were due to program participation rather than other factors. Based on the results of this review, the Study Group reported that among other things, there is a need for additional, methodologically rigorous evaluations of girls' delinquency programs; training and technical assistance to help programs prepare for evaluations; and funding to support girls' delinquency programs found to be promising. According to OJJDP officials, in response to the Study Group's finding about the need to better prepare programs for evaluation, the office plans to work with the group and use the remaining funding from the effort—approximately $300,000—to provide technical assistance workshop in October 2009. The workshop is intended to help approximately 10 girls' delinquency programs prepare for evaluation by providing information about how evaluations are designed and conducted, how to identify appropriate performance measures, and how to collect data that will be useful for program evaluators in assessing outcomes. In addition, OJJDP officials stated that as a result of the Study Group's findings along with feedback they received from members of the girls' delinquency field, OJJDP plans to issue a solicitation in early fiscal year 2010 for researchers to apply for funding to conduct evaluations of two to five girls' delinquency programs. OJJDP has also reported that the Study Group's findings are to provide a foundation for moving ahead on a comprehensive program related to girls' delinquency. However, OJJDP has not developed a plan that is documented, is shared with key stakeholders, and includes specific funding requirements and commitments and time frames for meeting its girls' delinquency goals. Standard practices for program and project management state that specific desired outcomes or results should be conceptualized, defined, and documented in the planning process as part of a road map, along with the appropriate projects needed to achieve those results, supporting resources, and milestones.[13] In addition, government internal control standards call for policies and procedures that establish adequate communication with stakeholders as essential for achieving desired program goals.[14] According to OJJDP officials, they have not developed such a plan because the office is in transition and is in the process of initiating efforts to develop an officewide research plan, but they are taking steps to address their girls' delinquency goals, for example, through the workshop and planned evaluations. Developing such a plan would help OJJDP to demonstrate leadership to the girls' delinquency field by clearly articulating the actions it intends to take to meet its goals and would also help the office to ensure that the goals are met.

To help ensure that OJJDP meets its goals to identify effective or promising girls' delinquency programs and supports the development of program models, we are recommending that the Administrator of OJJDP develop and document a plan that (1) articulates how the office intends to respond to the findings of the Study Group, (2) includes time frames and specific funding requirements and commitments, and (3) is shared with key stakeholders. In commenting on a draft of this report, OJP agreed with our recommendation and outlined efforts that OJJDP plans to undertake to respond to the findings of the Study Group, which we describe in the report. OJP comments are reprinted in the enclosure.

BACKGROUND

Over the past two decades girls have increasingly become involved in the juvenile justice system, and while the majority of juvenile arrests and cases involve boys, research has indicated that girls have more intensive treatment needs than boys. In 1980, 20 percent of all juvenile arrests were girls; by the mid-1990s about one quarter of these arrests were girls; and by 2007, girls accounted for 29 percent of all juvenile arrests. Additionally, while arrests for some violent crimes, such as assaults, have decreased for males, they have decreased less, or in some cases have increased, for females. For example, between 1998 and 2007 juvenile male arrests for simple assault declined 4 percent, and female arrests increased 10 percent.[15] Further, from 1985 through 2005, the estimated number of girls' delinquency cases involving detention increased by 92 percent, and those cases that involved probation increased by 88 percent. Research on girls has highlighted that delinquent girls have higher rates of mental health problems than delinquent boys, receive fewer special services, and are more likely to abandon treatment programs. For example, one study showed that detained girls have more symptoms of mental illness than would be predicted on the basis of gender or setting alone.[16] Research has also shown that delinquent girls have higher mortality rates, dysfunctional and violent relationships, poor educational achievement, and less stable work histories than nondelinquent girls. Further, girls' delinquency has been linked to drug abuse, mental health problems and disorders, poorer physical health, and victimization by and violence toward partners in adulthood.

In recent years, programs have been developed that specifically target preventing girls' delinquency and intervening once girls have become involved in the juvenile justice system. In general, prevention programs provide services and programming, such as substance abuse education, mentoring, and life skills education, to deter girls from becoming involved in criminal or other antisocial activities. Intervention programs provide services to girls once they have entered the juvenile justice system, for example, through programs that are alternatives to probation or that provide intensive services for girls who are on probation, to prevent them from returning to the system or entering the adult criminal justice system. These services could include visits by probation officers, individual case plans, substance abuse treatment and therapy, funds for emergency situations, life skills courses, teen pregnancy services, and therapy sessions.

The Juvenile Justice and Delinquency Prevention Act (the Act) established OJJDP in 1974.[17] As the only federal office charged exclusively with preventing and responding to juvenile delinquency and victimization and with helping states improve their juvenile justice systems, OJJDP supports its mission through a variety of activities, including: funding research and evaluation efforts, statistical studies, and demonstration programs; providing training and technical assistance; producing and distributing publications and other products containing information about juvenile justice topics; and administering a wide variety of grants to states, territories, localities, and public and private organizations through formula, block, and discretionary grant programs.[18] Table 1 shows OJJDP's enacted appropriations for fiscal years 2007 through 2009.

Table 1. Juvenile Justice Appropriations Fiscal Years 2007 through 2009

Dollars in thousands			
Line item	Funding by fiscal year		
	2007	2008	2009
Part A – Concentration of Federal Efforts[a]	$703	$658	$0
Part B – State Formula Grants	78,976	74,260	75,000
Part D—Research, Evaluation, Technical Assistance and Training	0	0	0
Part E – Developing, Testing and Demonstrating Promising New Initiatives and Projects	104,670	93,835	82,000
Youth Mentoring Grants	9,872	70,000	80,000
Title V – Local Delinquency Prevention Incentive Grants	64,168	61,100	62,000
Project Childsafe[b]	987	0	0
Secure Our Schools	14,808	15,040	0
VOCA—Improving Investigation and Prosecution of Child Abuse Program	14,808	16,920	20,000
Juvenile Accountability Block Grant Program[c]	49,360	51,700	55,000
Total	**$338,352**	**$383,513**	**$374,000**

Sources: Revised Continuing Appropriations Resolution, 2007, Pub. L. No. 110-5, 121 Stat. 8, 8-9 (including the across-the-board rescission of 1.28 percent provided in the continuing resolution); Consolidated Appropriations Act, 2008, Pub. L. No. 110-161, 121 Stat. 1844, 1911-12 (2007); and Omnibus Appropriations Act, 2009, Pub. L. No. 111-8, 123 Stat. 524, 581-82.

[a] According to OJP's fiscal year 2010 congressional budget submission, the Concentration of Federal Efforts program promotes interagency cooperation and coordination among federal agencies with responsibilities in the area of juvenile justice, as authorized by Part A of the Act, as amended.

[b] Project Childsafe is a nationwide program to promote safe firearms handling and storage practices through the distribution of safety education messages and free gun-locking devices.

[c] Under the Juvenile Accountability Block Grant Program, OJJDP provides funds to states and units of local government for the purpose of strengthening the juvenile justice system. These funds can be used for 17 different purpose areas, including establishing programs to help the successful reentry of juvenile offenders from state and local custody in the community or for hiring or training programs for detention and corrections personnel.

OJJDP, through its various grant programs, has provided funding to states and organizations to support girls' delinquency programs, although it is not specifically required by the Act to fund such programs in particular. For example, to be eligible to receive formula grants, states are required to submit a plan to OJJDP for providing gender-specific services for juvenile delinquency prevention and treatment.[19] However, the states generally have the authority to determine how formula and block grants are allocated and may use these funds to support a range of program areas, including programs specifically for delinquent girls. For example, for fiscal years 2007 and 2008, OJJDP reported that states used approximately $1.9 million in Part B formula grant money for girls' delinquency programs, representing approximately 1 percent of such funding for those years. In addition, in fiscal year 2007, OJJDP reported awarding about $1.8 million in discretionary grant awards to prevention and intervention programs addressing girls' delinquency.[20]

The Act requires the OJJDP Administrator to conduct and support evaluations and studies of the performance and results achieved by federal juvenile delinquency programs and activities, although the law does not specifically require OJJDP to fund evaluations of state or locally funded programs or those specifically focused on girls' delinquency.[21] OJJDP has provided funding for evaluations using (1) funds appropriated for Part D of the Act—which allows the Administrator to conduct research and evaluation, information dissemination, and training and technical assistance,[22] or (2) funds set aside from several of its appropriations accounts for use for research, evaluation, and statistics activities.[23] Funding has not been appropriated to OJJDP for Part D since fiscal year 2005 when it received $10 million, so OJJDP has allocated funding for research and evaluation of programs from fiscal years 2006 through 2008 using approximately $40 million in funding from appropriation set asides.[24]

OJJDP has provided funding for several efforts designed to provide information about girls' delinquency programs to the juvenile justice field in the past decade. For example, in 1998, the office published an inventory of best practices that included a list of 16 promising girls' delinquency programs, which had been compiled by a research organization as part of a $1.1 million cooperative agreement to provide training and technical assistance to states and localities about girls' programs.[25] The research organization identified these 16 programs on the basis of programmatic criteria—such as whether the program used appropriate assessments to determine treatment plans; provided empowerment strategies, such as skill training and vocational training; or provided its staff with gender-specific training—rather than on whether the program's effectiveness had been studied by researchers. Further, this effort found that more research was needed to draw conclusions about the effectiveness of girls' delinquency program models. In addition, during this time OJJDP spent approximately $1.1 million to fund four studies of girls' delinquency issues. While these studies assessed issues related to girls' delinquency, they did not specifically assess the effectiveness of girls' delinquency programs. For example, in 2000, OJJDP funded one study of women in gangs, which found, among other things, that the optimum time for prevention and intervention was the middle teen years and that the optimum place for intervention was school before girls drop out. Another study compared three treatment models to determine which was most effective at reducing the number of institutional placements for adjudicated female offenders. The study found that girls with the most serious and frequent crises were more dissatisfied with social services or were denied access to such services. The study highlighted the importance of youth assistance programs to provide opportunities for girls to develop pro-social skills through family, school, and community connections.

OJJDP ESTABLISHED THE GIRLS STUDY GROUP TO ASSESS THE EFFECTIVENESS OF GIRLS' DELINQUENCY PROGRAMS

OJJDP, initiated the Study Group to assess the effectiveness of girls' delinquency programs. In response to increases in girls' arrests through the 1990s and early 2000s and questions about the causes of these increases and how best to respond to the needs of girls entering the juvenile justice system, OJJDP issued a program announcement in 2003 for a study group to focus on girls' delinquency issues.[26] While OJJDP had funded studies on girls' issues and a technical assistance effort to assist girls' delinquency programs in their operations, in forming the Study Group, OJJDP determined that a comprehensive, research-based foundation was needed to guide state and local policymakers and practitioners in their efforts to effectively prevent and reduce girls' delinquency. In its announcement for the Study Group, OJJDP highlighted the need for more information about female development and female-specific delinquency risk factors, as well as the effectiveness of girls' delinquency programs to ensure the best services and treatment. OJJDP sought applications from public and private organizations to convene a study group to address these issues and in 2004 awarded a 2-year cooperative agreement to Research Triangle Institute (RTI) to do so. OJJDP has since provided RTI with an extension through June 2010 to complete all of the Study Group's activities. The total funding awarded for the cooperative agreement was almost $2.6 million.

OJJDP articulated five broad objectives for the Study Group in its September 2003 program announcement. Three of these objectives specifically related to assessing and promoting girls' delinquency programs: (1) identifying effective or promising programs, program, elements, and implementation principles to help inform communities about what works in preventing or reducing girls' delinquency and to support the development of these program models; (2) identifying gaps in girls' delinquency research and developing recommendations for future research to fill these gaps; and (3) disseminating findings to the girls' delinquency field about effective or promising programs. The other two objectives included understanding the trends and consequences related to girls' delinquency and developing a comprehensive theory of girls' delinquency.[27]

To meet OJJDP's program assessment objectives, among other activities, the Study Group conducted a review of the literature on girls' delinquency that included over 1,000 documents in relevant research areas, such as criminological and feminist explanations for girls' delinquency, patterns of delinquency, and the justice system's response to girls' delinquency. To identify girls' delinquency programs, from June 2005 through October 2006, the Study Group analyzed the results of this literature search, conducted Web searches, reviewed juvenile justice 3-year plans from 2000 to 2004 for all 50 states, reviewed federal agency and private organization lists of delinquency programs, and solicited suggestions on its Web site.[28] The Study Group initially set out to identify federally funded girls' delinquency programs but expanded its search to include state and locally funded programs after it found few federally funded programs. As a result, the Study Group identified 61 programs that specifically targeted preventing or responding to girls' delinquency. The group then determined which of these programs had been studied for program effectiveness by conducting Web searches for evaluation materials and published research, reviewing abstracts from academic journals, contacting program directors, and reviewing program Web sites.

To identify effective programs, the Study Group reviewed the studies of girls' delinquency programs that it identified and classified them based on evidence of their effectiveness. To make this determination, the Study Group compared the studies' methodologies to criteria established in the OJP What

Works classification framework, which defines six levels of evidence of effectiveness, which are effective, effective with reservation, promising, and ineffective, as well as inconclusive evidence and insufficient evidence, as described in table 2.[29]

Table 2. Summary of What Works Criteria Used by the Girls Study Group to Assess Studies of Girls' Delinquency Programs

Level of effectiveness	Description
Effective	Effective programs have studies with a randomized controll-ed research design. These are designs that compare the outcomes for individuals that are randomly assigned either to the program or to a nonparticipating control group before the intervention in an effort to control for any systematic diff-erence between the groups that could account for a differ-ence in their outcomes. Effective programs also demonstrate a significant and sustained effect—that is, statistically significant positive outcomes that remain for at least 1 year after subjects stop participating in a program. The program should have been replicated at least once externally at another site to confirm results.
Effective with reservation	These programs have studies with a randomized controlled research design that demonstrates a significant and sustained effect. A program should have at least one replication to confirm results. Reservations occur either because the program has only an internal replication at the same site or because it has an external replication with modest results.
Promising	Promising programs have either studies with (1) a rando-mized controlled research design without a replication or (2) a quasi-experimental research design. These programs have significant and sustained effects.
Insufficient evidence	These are studies of programs that have a quasi-experimental research design that lack sufficient methodological rigor, or have a pre-post test design that involves tests that analyze measures before and after individuals participated in the program.
Inconclusive evidence	These studies of programs may have adequately rigorous research designs but not sustained effects, or they may have contradictory findings and not enough evidence demons-trating that the programs are either effective or ineffective.
Ineffective	These are studies of programs that have an experimental or quasi-experimental research design that failed to demon-strate a significant effect in an initial study or in a replication.

Source: GAO analysis of OJP What Works criteria.

According to the Study Group's principal investigator, as of May 2009, the group had finalized its program review findings and was in the process of finishing a bulletin on these findings before providing it to OJJDP for publication. As of June 2009, OJJDP has issued three bulletins on several of the group's activities. These bulletins have provided an overview of the Study Group's activities and the group's findings on its two objectives related to girls' delinquency risk factors and patterns of offending. According to OJJDP officials, the Study Group plans to issue a final report that summarizes all of its activities and findings to OJJDP by spring 2010.

OJJDP Efforts to Assess Program Effectiveness Were Consistent with Social Science Practices and Standards, and OJJDP Has Taken Action to Enhance Its Communication about Study Group Activities and Findings with External Stakeholders

OJJDP's efforts to assess program effectiveness through the use of a study group as well as the group's efforts were consistent with generally accepted social science practices and standards, although experts we interviewed presented differing views on the criteria used to assess programs. OJJDP also took action to include external stakeholders in study group activities and is disseminating the group's findings consistent with standards for control in the federal government.

The Use of a Study Group and the Group's Efforts Were Consistent with Generally Accepted Social Science Practices and Standards; However, Experts We Interviewed Presented Differing Views on the Criteria Used to Assess Programs

OJJDP's efforts to assess girls' delinquency programs, including its approach of using a study group and the group's methods of assessing studies, were consistent with generally accepted social science standards for evaluation research. According to OJJDP officials, including the research coordinator, they chose to form a study group rather than fund individual evaluations of programs because study groups are a cost-effective method of gaining an overview of the available research in an issue area. As part of its work, the group collected, reviewed, and analyzed the methodological quality of research on girls' delinquency programs. Such an approach of systematically identifying and reviewing research conducted in a field of study is an acceptable practice to consolidate the research in an area and provide information to enable program managers to determine where they might best commit future evaluation resources.[30] Thirteen of the 18 girls' delinquency experts we interviewed (including 11 Study Group members) stated that the Study Group's efforts were useful for providing an overview of girls' delinquency issues. However, 6 experts (including 2 Study Group members) also noted that it would have been beneficial to the girls' delinquency field for the group to conduct evaluations to determine program outcomes or promising models rather than reviewing completed studies. OJJDP has funded individual studies of girls' delinquency programs in the past but, according to OJJDP officials, was seeking to use the Study Group's research to form a baseline of the available knowledge about girls' delinquency issues.

The Study Group's effort to review the studies according to the What Works criteria was consistent with generally accepted social science standards. Specifically, we reviewed the OJP What Works criteria and found that they adhere to these standards for evaluation research. Using the What Works criteria, we also assessed the same studies for the 17 girls' delinquency programs that the Study Group had reviewed and generally concurred with the Study Group's ratings of the program studies. While the Study Group's use of the What Works criteria was in keeping with social science standards, experts we interviewed expressed differing views on the group's decision to use these criteria. According to the Study Group's former principal investigator, the group decided to use the What Works criteria in 2005 because the criteria ensured that the group's assessment of the effectiveness of programs in preventing or reducing girls' delinquency would be based on highly rigorous evaluation standards to identify effective programs— thus eliminating the potential that a program that may do harm would be endorsed by the group. Eight Study Group members we interviewed also stated that the Study Group's use of the criteria was appropriate because it ensured that the group would only disseminate information on programs determined to be effective based on a high level of evidence. However, 8 other experts, including three Study Group members, said that the criteria created an unrealistically high standard, which caused the Study Group to overlook potentially promising programs.[31] Further, 9 of the 18 experts (including five Study Group members) we interviewed also noted that requiring a randomized controlled research design—a research design that compares the outcomes for individuals who are randomly assigned to either the program being studied or to a nonparticipating control group before the intervention—to demonstrate effectiveness, as the What Works criteria does, is a difficult standard to achieve because such a design is expensive, and programs may be reluctant to divert resources from programming to pay for evaluations. OJJDP officials stated that they understood the experts' concerns and the trade-offs in using a classification framework that requires a randomized controlled research design to demonstrate effectiveness; however, they approved the group's use of the criteria because it provided a rigorous framework for assessing program evaluations. We understand that studies can produce valid results using other research designs, such as studies using quasi-experimental designs or studies comparing the outcome results for groups of girls that are statistically matched. We have also previously reported that randomized controlled research designs provide researchers with the best method for assessing a program's effectiveness—they isolate changes caused by the program from other factors—when doing so is feasible and ethical.[32]

OJJDP Has Taken Actions to Reach Out to External Stakeholders on Study Group Activities and Findings and Is Disseminating the Findings in Keeping with Internal Control Standards

OJJDP has taken action to reach out to external stakeholders to address concerns about the composition of the Study Group after its initial formation and, moving forward, plans to continue to incorporate program practitioners in its planned efforts. *Standards for Internal Control in the Federal Government* states that program managers should ensure that there are adequate means of obtaining information from and communicating with external stakeholders who may have a significant impact on the agency achieving its goals.[33] Regarding gaining information from external stakeholders, OJJDP's program announcement for the Study Group sought to ensure a range of stakeholder perspectives related to girls' delinquency. The announcement required that the members of the Study Group possess knowledge of and experience with female development and delinquent girls and demonstrate expertise in a variety of relevant social science disciplines, such as criminology, sociology, and developmental psychology. In awarding the cooperative agreement to RTI through a peer review process, OJJDP approved the RTI proposal for the Study Group as responding to the requirements and expectations of the program announcement. Consistent with the fields of expertise cited in the program announcement, RTI convened a group of 13 members, including 12 academic researchers from social science disciplines and one practitioner, a member directly involved in girls' delinquency programming.[34] However, according to several of the experts we interviewed, this Study Group composition did not include sufficient representation and input from a key external stakeholders group—girls' delinquency program practitioners. For example, 11 of the 18 girls' delinquency experts we interviewed, including 5 study group members, said that the Study Group was imbalanced in favor of academic researchers, 6 of whom (including 2 study group members) said that the composition led the group to focus its efforts on researching theories of girls' delinquency rather than gathering and disseminating actionable information for practitioners.[35] According to OJJDP officials we interviewed, they had received feedback from girls' delinquency stakeholders in 2006 on this issue. In response, according to OJJDP program managers, they acted to address the imbalance of the Study Group by adding a second practitioner as a member and involving 2 other practitioners in group activities, such as presenting successful girls' delinquency program practices at conferences and reviewing the group's work products.[36] OJJDP officials stated that as a lesson learned, they plan to more fully involve practitioners from the beginning when they organize study groups in the future. In addition, OJJDP officials noted that specific to the Study Group, they plan to continue to reach out to obtain information from and include practitioners in the remaining activities of the group, such as presenting findings at a national juvenile justice conference.

OJJDP and the Study Group have disseminated the group's findings to the research community, practitioners in the girls' delinquency field, and the public in a variety of ways, and in doing so have made efforts to respond to stakeholder concerns. In its 2003 program announcement, in keeping with the internal control standard for communicating with stakeholders, OJJDP required that the Study Group disseminate its findings through publications and products that address the needs of various practitioner audiences in diverse fields, including juvenile justice, child welfare, mental health, and substance abuse prevention. Since 2004, Study Group principal investigators and group members have presented findings at 24 conferences and posted the presentation slides to the group's Web site.[37] OJJDP has also published three bulletins on the Study Group's activities and findings. Six girls' delinquency experts we interviewed (including five Study Group members) stated that the information disseminated was generally helpful because it provided a useful overview of girls' delinquency trends and research.

However, 10 of the 18 experts we interviewed (including three Study Group members) also noted that some of the group's dissemination efforts created confusion among practitioners because Study Group members presented findings that did not acknowledge factors that practitioners believed contribute to girls' delinquency, such as traumatic life experiences. According to OJJDP officials, in response to feedback they received from girls' delinquency stakeholders about such concerns, the office and the Study Group sponsored workshop sessions at a conference for juvenile justice practitioners where the group clarified its findings and sought practitioner input on subjects such as delinquency risk and protective factors and trends in girls' delinquency. According to OJJDP officials, the office and the Study Group plan to continue disseminating the group's findings by issuing four additional bulletins and by presenting the findings at a national conference on juvenile delinquency.

In Response to Study Group Findings of No Evidence of Effective Girls' Delinquency Programs, OJJDP Plans Technical Assistance to Help Programs but Could Strengthen Its Plans for Supporting Evaluations

The OJJDP-sponsored Study Group found that no programs in its review had evidence of effectiveness and, among other things, that additional support for program evaluation is needed. To address these findings, OJJDP plans to provide technical assistance to help girls' delinquency programs so that they will be better prepared to be evaluated. However, by articulating time frames and specific funding requirements and commitments in its plans to support evaluations, OJJDP could better address its goals for preventing and reducing girls' delinquency.

The Study Group Found No Evidence of Effective Girls' Delinquency Programs to Promote as Models and, among Other Things, That Evaluation Is Needed

In its review of girls' delinquency programs, the Study Group's findings showed that the majority of the programs it identified—44 of 61—had not been studied by researchers, while 17 of the programs had been the subject of published studies. The Study Group determined that none of the 17 programs that had been studied had conclusive evidence of their effectiveness. Specifically, the Study Group found that the studies provided insufficient evidence of the effectiveness of 11 of these 17 programs. For example, our review of one study that the Study Group assessed as having insufficient evidence showed that the study had a quasi-experimental design but lacked methodological rigor in that the treatment and comparison groups had small sample sizes and did not appear to be well matched, and any statistical tests reported were only performed on treatment group participants.[38] The Study Group found that for the remaining 6 programs, the studies provided inconclusive evidence of effectiveness. For example, our review of one study that the group assessed as having inconclusive evidence showed statistically significant results for the program; however, sustained effects were not indicated for at least a 1-year period beyond the end of the intervention. Further, it was unclear whether the study participants were representative of the population of girls that the program was designed to reach. As a result, there was not enough evidence to demonstrate that the program was either effective or ineffective for the intended population of delinquent girls. Among the other findings that the Study Group reported was that 7 of the 17 programs it assessed were no longer in operation, primarily because the initial grants that supported their operations were not renewed.

Based on its review of girls' delinquency programs, the Study Group reported several conclusions and recommendations. Among these conclusions and recommendations is the need for evaluations and support of girls' delinquency programs. In particular, the Study Group found that insufficient funding has been provided for evaluations of girls' delinquency programs, so definitive conclusions of what works for girls cannot be made. Further, the Study Group found that additional, methodologically rigorous evaluations of girls' delinquency programs are needed in order to identify effective and promising programs and models that could be replicated at the state and local levels. While the Study Group did not specifically quantify the funding needed to support these evaluations, it did note that federal sources for evaluation funding and partnerships with local colleges and universities are needed. The Study Group also concluded that programs need technical assistance to help them prepare for evaluations. Lastly, the group found that girls' delinquency programs that are based on evidence of promising techniques should be supported and expanded. In particular, the Study Group highlighted program sustainability as an issue, stating that funding needs to be provided to ensure that the most promising programs continue to operate after their initial funding period is over so that practitioners and policymakers can continue to implement them.

OJJDP Plans to Provide Technical Assistance to Help Programs, but Could More Fully Develop Plans for Supporting Evaluations to Address Its Goals to Prevent and Reduce Girls' Delinquency

OJJDP has plans to provide technical assistance to girls' delinquency programs; however, its plans for supporting evaluations could be more fully developed to help OJJDP reach its goals for addressing girls' delinquency issues. OJJDP's goals for addressing girls' delinquency, as stated in the Study Group program announcement, are to identify effective and promising programs, program elements, and implementation principles and support the development of program models to prevent and reduce girls' delinquency. According to OJJDP officials, in response to the group's finding about the need to better prepare programs for evaluation, the office plans to work with the Study Group and using the remainder of its funding—approximately $300,000—provide a technical assistance workshop in October 2009 to help about 10 girls' delinquency programs prepare to be evaluated. In this workshop, OJJDP and the Study Group plan to provide information to programs about how evaluations are designed and conducted, how to identify appropriate performance measures, and how to collect data needed for program evaluators to assess outcomes. OJJDP officials stated that the programs are to be selected for participation through an application process and have to meet minimum criteria, including having experience working with girls and the capability to collect program outcome data. OJJDP officials noted that they intend to limit participation in the workshop to about 10 programs to ensure that the programs that are selected receive technical assistance that is targeted to their specific needs. This assistance, according to OJJDP officials, will help ensure that when programs do undergo evaluations—whether funded by OJJDP, another federal agency, or an independent research organization—the evaluations will be more likely to lead to conclusive findings on program effectiveness.

In addition to providing girls' delinquency programs with training and technical assistance, OJJDP officials also described their plan to fund evaluations of girls' delinquency programs. OJJDP officials stated that as a result of the Study Group's findings along with feedback they received from members of the girls' delinquency field, they recognized the need for evaluations of girls' delinquency programs. OJJDP officials stated that they recognized the need for evaluation in fiscal year 2007 but at the time lacked funding to issue a solicitation for such evaluations. Further, 14 of the 18 girls' delinquency experts that we interviewed (including nine Study Group members) emphasized the need for OJJDP leadership in supporting evaluations of girls' delinquency programs to identify effective programs. For example, one expert noted that since the Study Group found that few programs had been studied, OJJDP would be doing a disservice to the girls' delinquency field if it did not fund rigorous evaluations and help programs partner with research organizations. According to the OJJDP officials, the office's goal is to issue a solicitation in early fiscal year 2010 for researchers to apply for funding to conduct evaluations of two to five girls' delinquency programs. These evaluations, according to OJJDP officials, are to focus on girls' delinquency programs that have been in operation for a number of years and have data to support evaluations. The officials also stated that the planned solicitation would require researchers to conduct studies that involve either randomized controlled or quasi-experimental research designs.

OJJDP officials stated that they expect to fund evaluations using the portion of appropriation accounts that has been available for research and evaluations, and noted that the number of evaluations to be allocated funding depends, in part, on the number of applications received, the total available funding, as well as other competing research needs and goals. While OJJDP has not yet received an appropriation for fiscal year 2010, OJJDP used approximately \$12 million in fiscal year 2007 and \$14 million in fiscal year 2008 to support research and evaluations from accounts eligible to support research and evaluations of girls' delinquency programs. OJJDP officials stated that they used this funding because in recent years they have not received an appropriation for programs and activities authorized under Part D, which is specifically designated for research and evaluation, but if they were to receive a Part D appropriation they could increase the number of evaluations funded. While OJJDP officials verbally described the planned evaluations and funding, they did not provide us with written documentation of the planned solicitation because, as of June 2009, it was in draft and subject to change.

OJJDP officials have described actions they plan to take to respond to the Study Group's findings, and OJJDP reported that these findings will provide a foundation for creating a comprehensive program of information dissemination, training, technical assistance, and programming to help prevent and reduce girls' delinquency. However, the office has not developed a plan that is documented, is shared with key stakeholders, and includes time frames and specific funding requirements and commitments for meeting its girls' delinquency goals. According to OJJDP officials, they have not developed such a plan because the office is in transition and is in the process of initiating efforts to develop an officewide research plan, but they are taking steps to address their girls' delinquency goals, for example, through the workshop and planned evaluations. Standard practices for program and project management state that specific desired outcomes or results should be conceptualized, defined, and documented in the planning process as part of a road map, along with the appropriate projects needed to achieve those results, supporting resources, and milestones.[39] *Standards for Internal Control in the Federal Government* states that program managers should ensure that there are adequate means of obtaining information from and communicating with external stakeholders who may have a significant impact on the agency achieving its goals.[40] We have also previously reported that critical to guiding evaluation and research efforts on a national level is a strategy that outlines a process for funding and conducting rigorous evaluations and research, identifies the resources needed to achieve it, and assigns accountability for accomplishing these actions.[41] In that regard, developing a plan that provides a road map to meeting its goals would provide additional assurance that OJJDP's goals for identifying and promoting promising programs and program models would be met and communicated to state and local policymakers and practitioners responsible for implementing programs to prevent and reduce girls' delinquency.

CONCLUSIONS

Preventing and responding to girls' delinquency have been a concern for federal, state, and local governments as well as private and nonprofit juvenile justice organizations for over a decade, and the most recent statistics show that girls' involvement in the juvenile justice system is not stabilizing or declining. While OJJDP has undertaken a 6-year, $2.6 million study group effort to learn about effective and promising girls' delinquency programs, the lack of rigorous studies of such programs meant that the group was unable to identify and promote effective programs and to develop program models to be supported at state and local levels. In response to these findings, OJJDP has taken steps to provide technical assistance to programs to help prepare them for evaluations and has described plans for funding evaluations of girls' delinquency programs. While these steps are consistent with OJJDP's stated goals, the office lacks a comprehensive documented plan that includes time frames and specific funding requirements and commitments for meeting its girls' delinquency goals that it can share with stakeholders. As the Study Group plans to conclude its efforts in spring 2010, OJJDP is planning to help ensure the development of effective girls' delinquency programs and program models by providing training and technical assistance to help these programs plan for future evaluations. Moreover, such action better positions OJJDP in ensuring that funding for such programs is directed to those that are effective in preventing girls' delinquency and intervening after girls have entered the juvenile justice system. As states are continuing to make determinations about how to allocate their formula and block grants, and OJJDP continues to provide funding to programs through some of its discretionary grant programs, information about promising or effective programs and program models could help guide these resource decisions. Developing a plan with time frames that clearly articulates the office's approach to its evaluation efforts, including available resources needed and committed toward implementing that plan, would help OJJDP ensure that its goals to support the development of effective programs are met, and sharing that plan with stakeholders would help demonstrate federal leadership to the girls' delinquency field.

RECOMMENDATION FOR EXECUTIVE ACTION

To help ensure that OJJDP meets its goals to identify effective or promising girls' delinquency programs and supports the development of program models, we recommend that the Administrator of OJJDP develop and document a plan that (1) articulates how the office intends to respond to the program findings of the Study Group, (2) includes time frames and specific funding requirements and commitments, and (3) is shared with key stakeholders.

AGENCY COMMENTS AND OUR EVALUATION

We requested comments on a draft of this report from the Attorney General. On July 16, 2009, we received written comments from OJP, which are reprinted in the enclosure.

OJP agreed with our recommendation and stated that OJJDP has always intended to respond to the findings of the Study Group. OJP described efforts planned in response to the findings of the Study Group, including a technical assistance workshop and evaluations, which we have discussed in our report. OJP also stated that subsequent refined plans and related funding commitments will be based on the outcome of these activities and noted that OJJDP, in accordance with the Act, will publish these program plans in the *Federal Register* for review and comment by key stakeholders as well as members of the public by December 2009.

We recognize that OJJDP's planned activities represent a worthwhile step in responding to the findings from the Study Group effort, and are encouraged that OJJDP intends to publish a program plan, to include how it will address girls' delinquency issues. However, it is important to note that while OJJDP has been required to publish a program plan annually according to the Act, it has not done so since 2002.[42] Following through on its current pledge to issue such a plan by December of this year will help provide OJJDP with reasonable assurance that it has a well-thought-out approach to ensure that its goals for preventing and reducing girls' delinquency are met. We also continue to maintain that it will be important for this plan to include more than a list of activities in response to the Study Group's findings as OJJDP describes in commenting on this report. Specifically, the plan should serve as a road map for OJJDP's approach for responding to the Study Group's findings, establish overall time frames as well as those for each activity, specify funding requirements and associated commitments, and integrate the input of key stakeholders, such as girls' delinquency practitioners. Publishing and implementing such a plan would help OJJDP ensure that it meets the goal it articulated at the beginning of the 6-year Study Group effort—to identify effective and promising programs, program elements, and implementation principles and to support the development of program models to prevent and reduce girls' delinquency.

We are sending copies of this report to interested congressional committees, the Attorney General, and other interested parties. In addition, this report will be available at no charge on GAO's Web site at http://www.gao.gov.

If you or your staff have any questions concerning this report, please contact me at (202) 512-6510 or larencee@gao.gov. Contact points for our Offices of Congressional Relations and Public Affairs may be found on the last page of this report. Mary Catherine Hult, Assistant Director; David Alexander; Elizabeth Blair; Amy Brown; Kevin Copping; Katherine Davis; Dawn Locke; and Janet Temko made key contributions to this report.

Sincerely yours,

Eileen Regen Larence

Eileen Regen Larence Director, Homeland Security and Justice Issues
Enclosure

COMMENTS FROM THE DEPARTMENT OF JUSTICE

U.S. Department of Justice

Office of Justice Programs

Office of Audit, Assessment, and Managemen

Washington, D.C. 20531

JUL 1 6 2009

Ms. Eileen R. Larence
Director, Homeland Security and Justice Issues
Government Accountability Office
441 G Street, NW
Washington, DC 20548

Dear Ms. Larence:

Thank you for the opportunity to comment on the draft Government Accountability
Office (GAO) letter report entitled "Juvenile Justice: Technical Assistance and Better
Defined Evaluation Plans Will Help to Improve Girls' Delinquency Programs" (GAO-09-
721R). The Office of Justice Programs agrees with the Recommendation for Executive
Action, which is restated in bold text below and is followed by our response.

**To help ensure that OJJDP meets its goals to identify effective or promising girls'
delinquency programs and supports the development of program models, we
recommend that the Administrator of OJJDP develop and document a plan, that
(1) articulates how the agency intends to respond to the program findings of the
Girls Study Group, (2) includes time frames and specific funding requirements and
commitments, and (3) is shared with key stakeholders.**

It has always been the intention of the Office of Juvenile Justice and Delinquency
Prevention (OJJDP) to respond to the findings of the Girls' Study Group. As discussed
with the GAO during the review, OJJDP has efforts underway, as well as planned
initiatives to address the findings. These planned initiatives, and timeframes for
implementation, are described below. Further planning and funding commitments will be
based on the outcome of these activities.

- **Hands-On Evaluation Technical Assistance Workshop for Girls' Delinquency
  Programs**

  The workshop is scheduled for October 28-30, 2009, in Chapel Hill, NC. The goal of
  the workshop is to better equip programs to conduct rigorous evaluations of their
  interventions. Unlike general workshops, the Girls' Study Group Evaluation
  Technical Assistance Workshop will tailor instruction specifically to address the
  needs of participating programs. The faculty at the workshops will be highly skilled
  in evaluation methodology, program development, and strategies on how to partner
  with evaluation professionals. Each participant will leave the workshop with a

customized concrete plan for 'next steps' and upon request will receive an additional hour of technical assistance by phone following the workshop.

Eligibility will be limited to programs that provide gender-responsive delinquency prevention or interventions for girls, and who have some level of evaluation experience. Organizations that have more than one distinct gender responsive program are eligible to submit more than one application. There will be a two-phase application process. The first phase will require the submission of general program information and a description of current evaluation history/experience. Program applications will be reviewed based on their program type and evaluation needs; and approximately 15 to 20 programs will be invited to proceed to the next application phase. Those applicants selected for the second phase will be asked to submit more detailed information on the evaluation needs of their programs and reports or findings based on previous evaluation work. The workshop organizers will use this information to determine which programs provide the best fit between evaluation needs and faculty expertise. Approximately 10 programs will ultimately be invited to participate in the workshop. Selection of participants for the workshop will be completed by the end of September 2009.

- **Enhancement of OJJDP's Current Girls Delinquency Training and Technical Assistance Curriculum**

  Using a panel of experts (including staff from the Girls' Study Group, among others), OJJDP will update, enhance, and revise the existing Training and Technical Assistance Curriculum for Girls' Delinquency Programming. The targeted completion date is December 2009.

- **Release of the FY 2010 Evaluation of Girls' Delinquency Programs Solicitation**

  This solicitation will be released, pending availability of funds, for the purpose of encouraging partnerships between girls' delinquency programs and evaluators, and providing funding for experimental and quasi-experimental evaluations of girls' delinquency programs.

In response to the findings of the Girls' Study Group, OJJDP has planned the above described initiatives. Subsequent refined plans and related funding commitments will be based on the outcome of these initiatives. As mandated by the Juvenile Justice and Delinquency Prevention Act, the OJJDP will publish these program plans in the Federal Register for review and comment by key stakeholders as well as members of the public. OJJDP anticipates publishing the program plan in the Federal Register by December 2009.

If you have any questions regarding this response, you or your staff may contact Maureen Henneberg, Director, Office of Audit, Assessment, and Management, on (202) 616-3282.

Sincerely,

Laurie O. Robinson
Acting Assistant Attorney General

cc: Beth McGarry
       Deputy Assistant Attorney for Operations and Management

       Jeffrey Slowikowski
       Acting Director
       Office of Juvenile Justice and Delinquency Prevention

       Maureen Henneberg
       Director
       Office of Audit, Assessment, and Management

       LeToya A. Johnson
       Audit Liaison
       Office of Justice Programs

       Richard P. Theis
       Audit Liaison
       Department of Justice

GAO's Mission

The Government Accountability Office, the audit, evaluation, and investigative arm of Congress, exists to support Congress in meeting its constitutional responsibilities and to help improve the performance and accountability of the federal government for the American people. GAO examines the use of public funds; evaluates federal programs and policies; and provides analyses, recommendations, and other assistance to help Congress make informed oversight, policy, and funding decisions. GAO's commitment to good government is reflected in its core values of accountability, integrity, and reliability.

End Notes

[1] C. Puzzanchera and W. Kang, *Juvenile Court Statistics Databook* (2008), http://ojjdp.ncjrs.gov/ojstatbb/jcsdb/ (accessed June 30, 2009). Most current data available.

[2] C. Puzzanchera, *Juvenile Arrests 2007*, (2009) www.ncjrs.gov/pdffiles1/ojjdp/225344.pdf (accessed June 26, 2009).

[3] The Federal Advisory Committee on Juvenile Justice is an advisory body established by the Juvenile Justice and Delinquency Prevention Act of 1974, as amended, to advise the President and Congress on state perspectives regarding the operation of the Office of Juvenile Justice and Delinquency Prevention and on federal legislation pertaining to juvenile justice and delinquency prevention, to advise the Administrator of the Office of Juvenile Justice and Delinquency Prevention, and to review federal policies regarding juvenile justice and delinquency prevention. 42 U.S.C. § 5633(f). The Federal Advisory Committee on Juvenile Justice comprises appointed representatives from each of the 50 states, the District of Columbia, and the 5 U.S. territories.

[4] Cooperative agreements, rather than grant awards, can be used by federal agencies when substantial involvement is expected between the agency and the recipient when carrying out the activities described in the program announcement.

[5] GAO defines an expert as a person who is recognized by others who work in the same subject matter area as having knowledge that is greater in scope or depth than that of most people working in that area. The expert's knowledge can come from education, experience, or both. We specifically identified researchers who focus on girls' delinquency issues and practitioners who operate programs that address girls' delinquency.

[6] We contacted all 15 of the study group members. However, 1 member declined to be interviewed, and 3 study group members did not respond to requests for interviews.

[7] For social science standards for evaluation research, see Donald T. Campbell and Julian Stanley, *Experimental and Quasi-Experimental Designs for Research* (Chicago: Rand McNally, 1963); William R. Shadish, Thomas D. Cook, and Donald T. Campbell, *Experimental and Quasi-Experimental Designs for Generalized Causal Inference* (Boston: Houghton Mifflin, 2002); Carol H. Weiss, *Evaluation: Methods for Studying Programs and Policies*, Second Edition (Englewood Cliffs, N.J.: Prentice-Hall, Inc., 1998); and GAO, *Designing Evaluations*, GAO/PEMD-10.1.4 (Washington, D.C.: May 1991).

[8] GAO, *Standards for Internal Control in the Federal Government*, GAO/AIMD-00-21.3.1 (Washington, D.C.: November 1999).

[9] Program management standards we reviewed are reflected in the Project Management Institute's *The Standard for Program Management* © (2006).

[10] The What Works criteria define six levels of effectiveness, including effective, promising, and ineffective, for use in assessing and classifying studies on the basis of their evidence of effectiveness. Additional details on these criteria are discussed later in this report.

[11] GAO/AIMD-00-21.3.1.

[12] The other seven experts did not express views regarding the balance of the study group's composition.

[13] Project Management Institute, *The Standard for Program Management*.

[14] GAO/AIMD-00-21.3.1.

[15] The Study Group found that possible reasons for increased arrest rates for girls include changes in local law enforcement policies that lowered the threshold for reporting assaults or categorizing assaults as aggravated, reclassification of domestic dispute offenses as simple assaults that can result in arrest, and increased referrals to police resulting from schools' zero tolerance policies for violence.

[16] Elizabeth Cauffman and others, "Gender Differences in Mental Health Symptoms among Delinquent and Community Youth," *Youth Violence and Juvenile Justice*, vol. 5, no. 3 (2007): 287–307.

[17] 42 U.S.C. § 5611.

[18] OJJDP allocates some formula and block grants to states on the basis of states' juvenile populations, while others may be awarded on the basis of a fixed level to all states. Discretionary grants are generally awarded through a competitive process to state and local governments as well as individual agencies and organizations. Under the Act, "state" means any of the United States, the District of Columbia, the Commonwealth of Puerto Rico, the Virgin Islands, Guam, American Samoa, and the Commonwealth of the Northern Mariana Islands. 42 U.S.C. § 5603.

[19] 42 U.S.C. § 5633(a)(7)(B).

[20] OJJDP did not report awarding discretionary grants for girls' programs in fiscal year 2008, and as of June 2009, OJJDP had not awarded fiscal year 2009 discretionary grants.

[21] 42 U.S.C. § 5614(b)(3).

[22] 42 U.S.C. §§ 5661-62.

[23] Appropriations statutes for fiscal years 2006 through 2008 provided that OJJDP may use not more than 10 percent of each amount appropriated for research, evaluation, and statistics activities that benefit the programs or activities authorized, and not more than 2 percent of each appropriated amount for training and technical assistance. *See, e.g,* Consolidated Appropriations Act, 2008, Pub. L. No. 110-161, 121 Stat. 1844, 1906-07 (2007). This provision applied to appropriation accounts under Juvenile Justice Programs, but did not apply to amounts appropriated for demonstration projects, as authorized by sections 261 and 262 of the Act, 42 U.S.C. §§ 5665-66.

[24] The $40 million comprises set asides eligible to be used for research and evaluation of girls' delinquency programs. As of July 2009, OJJDP has not determined how it would use its fiscal year 2009 appropriation set asides.

[25] Greene, Peters Associates, *Guiding Principles for Promising Female Programming: An Inventory of Best Practices* (Washington, D.C.: Office of Juvenile Justice and Delinquency Prevention, 1998).

[26] In 2000, OJJDP issued program announcements for two separate girls' delinquency efforts—a study group and a girls' institute. The first effort, a girls study group, was awarded to a university in 2001. However, because it was unable to reach agreement on project management issues, the university terminated the agreement in 2002. In 2003, OJJDP reissued the program announcement for a girls study group and revised the announcement to clearly delineate the level of expected federal involvement, for example, by explicitly stating that OJJDP planned to review and approve all project consultants, plans, and products developed. The second effort, a national girls' institute, was intended to put the study group's findings into practice by, among other things, promoting programs for girls; providing training and technical assistance to the field on girls' delinquency issues; facilitating coordination among federal, state, and local organizations serving girls; and disseminating information about the research findings of the study group. According to OJJDP officials, the 2000 announcement never received funding, and OJJDP did not reissue it in later years because of funding constraints. Instead, when OJJDP reissued the program announcement in 2003 for a study group, it incorporated elements of the planned institute. For example, the 2003 study group solicitation included objectives for identifying and promoting programs for girls and for disseminating information to the practitioner field.

[27] Specifically, the Study Group's objective to understand the trends and consequences of girls' delinquency involved increasing research-based knowledge about the risk and protective factors related to girls' delinquency and determining the patterns and consequences of juvenile justice decisions on female offenders. The objective on developing a comprehensive theory of girls' delinquency involved examining the extent to which theories developed primarily to explain boys' delinquency applied to girls, as well as exploring whether theories that had been developed for girls were useful in developing and testing new prevention and intervention strategies.

[28] Under the Act, states are required to submit 3-year plans to OJJDP outlining their activities for investing in delinquency prevention and for coordinating services delivered to at-risk juveniles and their families, among other things. 42 U.S.C. § 5633.

[29] A multiagency working group led by DOJ's OJP, which included the Department of Health and Human Services and the Department of Education, developed the classification framework and criteria from 2004 to 2005 to support a planned What Works repository to assist communities in selecting and replicating evidence-based programs that was never implemented. Federal government efforts to develop repositories of evidence-based programs have continued under Find Youth Info, the Substance Abuse and Mental Health Services Administration's National Registry of Evidence-Based Programs and Practices, and the OJJDP Model Programs Guide. Even though the repository was never implemented, the criteria within its framework are still valid to use in assessing evidence of program effectiveness.

[30] The approach used by OJJDP is similar to the evaluation synthesis methodology described in GAO, *The Evaluation Synthesis*, GAO/PEMD-10.1.2 (Washington, D.C.: March 1992). This type of approach might also be termed systematic review.

[31] Two experts we interviewed did not express a view on the group's approach to evaluating programs.

[32] GAO, *Juvenile Justice: OJJDP Reporting Requirements for Discretionary and Formula Grantees and Concerns About Evaluation Studies*, GAO-02-23 (Washington, D.C.: Oct. 30, 2001); *Justice Outcome Evaluations: Design and Implementation of Studies Require More NIJ Attention*, GAO-03-1091 (Washington, D.C.: Sept. 24, 2003); *Adult Drug Courts: Evidence Indicates Recidivism Reductions and Mixed Results for Other Outcomes*, GAO-05-219 (Washington, D.C.: Feb. 28, 2005); and *Abstinence Education: Assessing the Accuracy and Effectiveness of Federally Funded Programs*, GAO-08-664T (Washington, D.C.: Apr. 23, 2008).

[33] GAO/AIMD-00-21.3.1.

[34] The Study Group members represented 11 of the 12 disciplines specified in the program announcement.

[35] The other seven experts did not express views regarding the balance of the study group's composition.

[36] In addition to the practitioner, OJJDP also added an expert in program evaluation as a group member after the group had begun its activities.

[37] The Web site is located at http://girlsstudygroup.rti.org/index.cfm?fuseaction=dsp_home.

[38] A quasi-experimental design is a controlled study where study participants are assigned in a nonrandom manner to a treatment group (individuals participating in the program being studied) or a comparison group (individuals closely resembling those in the treatment group on many demographic variables but not participating in the program).

[39] Project Management Institute, *The Standard for Program Management*.

[40] GAO/AIMD-00-21.3.1.

[41] GAO, *South Florida Ecosystem Restoration: A Strategic Plan and a Process to Resolve Conflicts Are Needed to Keep the Effort on Track*, GAO/T-RCED-99-170 (Washington, D.C.: Apr. 29, 1999); *South Florida Ecosystem Restoration: Substantial Progress Made in Developing a Strategic Plan, but Actions Still Needed*, GAO-01-361 (Washington, D.C.: Mar. 27, 2001); and *Great Lakes: A Coordinated Strategic Plan and Monitoring System Are Needed to Achieve Restoration Goals*, GAO-03-999T (Washington, D.C.: July 16, 2003).

[42] 42 U.S.C. § 5614.

In: Not So Nice: Girls' Delinquency Issues   ISBN: 978-1-60876-268-2
Editor: Adam P. Mawer   © 2010 Nova Science Publishers, Inc.

Chapter 4

RESILIENT GIRLS - FACTOR THAT PROTECT AGAINST DELINQUENCY[*]

Stephanie R. Hawkins, Phillip W. Graham, Jason Williams and Margaret A. Zahn

According to data from the Federal Bureau of Investigation, from 1991 to 2000, arrests of girls increased more (or decreased less) than arrests of boys for most types of offenses. By 2004, girls accounted for 30 percent of all juvenile arrests. However, questions remain about whether these trends reflect an actual increase in girls' delinquency or changes in societal responses to girls' behavior. To find answers to these questions, the Office of Juvenile Justice and Delinquency Prevention (OJJDP) convened the Girls Study Group to establish a theoretical and empirical foundation to guide the development, testing, and dissemination of strategies to reduce or prevent girls' involvement in delinquency and violence.

The Girls Study Group Series, of which this Bulletin is a part, presents the Group's findings. The series examines issues such as patterns of offending among adolescents and how they differ for girls and boys; risk and protective factors associated with delinquency, including gender differences; and the causes and correlates of girls' delinquency.

---

[*] This is an edited, reformatted and augmented version of a U. S. Department of Justice publication dated January 2009.

Resilience, the psychological ability to successfully cope with severe stress and negative events, is a widely studied concept that has important implications for the development of delinquency prevention and intervention programs.

Despite the popularity of this concept in research, scientists still cannot completely explain why some children are resilient to the negative events and influences in their life while others are not. Furthermore, factors associated with resilience may not be the same for both genders.

Drawing on data from the National Longitudinal Study of Adolescent Health, this Bulletin examines a select number of factors that research suggests may "protect" girls who are at risk for becoming delinquent.

DEFINING RESILIENCE

Differences in conceptualizing resilience have led to confusion about what resilience really means (Luthar, Cicchetti, and Becker, 2000; Luthar and Zelazo, 2003; Olsson, Bond, and Burns, 2003). Resilience is often defined as a person's ability to positively adapt or achieve success despite having faced situations— being abused or neglected, witnessing violence, or living in poverty— that could lead to negative outcomes such as delinquency (Kaplan, 2005).

BACKGROUND

Developing the Study

Much of the research on resilience has focused on the risk factors that contribute to problem behaviors rather than on the factors that promote positive development (Smokowski, 1998). Although information on risk is important from a theoretical perspective, developing interventions focused on changing the risks for delinquent girls may not be the most effective approach. The knowledge that a girl is at risk for delinquency because she lives in a disadvantaged neighborhood or has a history of abuse is insufficient information for researchers and practitioners to develop an effective intervention program because these risk factors are not easily amenable to change in intervention programs (McKnight and Loper, 2002).

In view of the limitations of risk-focused intervention strategies, research on resilience turned toward protective factors—aspects of individuals and their environments that buffer or moderate the effect of risk (U.S. Department of Health and Human Services [DHHS], 2001; Fraser, Kirby, and Smokowski, 2004; Wright and Masten, 2005). The protective factors discussed in this Bulletin offer an explanation for why children and adolescents who face similar risk factors may or may not have a propensity toward negative outcomes like delinquency (DHHS, 2001).

The study described in this Bulletin was inspired in part by efforts to research factors that may protect against delinquency and to understand more clearly the unique needs and experiences of girls. Although many of the factors that place boys and girls at risk for delinquency are the same, current literature suggests that each sex may respond differently to protective factors (Resnick, Ireland, and Borowsky, 2004; Fraser, Kirby, and Smokowski, 2004). Research conducted by Resnick and colleagues found that grade point average (GPA) was the most salient protective factor against violence perpetration for both boys and girls, but family connectedness, school connectedness, and religiosity also provided significant protection against violence perpetration for girls only.

Reflecting these findings, this Bulletin explores four processes hypothesized to operate as protective factors in the lives of girls at risk for delinquency—support from or presence of a caring adult, school connected ness, school success, and religiosity.

Presence of a caring adult. Researchers have found that support from a caring adult can serve as a protective factor for adolescents, decreasing the likelihood that they will engage in delinquent behaviors (Dishion and Kavanagh, 2003; Romer, 2003; Benson, 1990; Hawley and DeHaan, 1996; Werner and Smith, 1982, 1992). Adolescents are less likely to engage in delinquent behaviors if they have adults in their lives who are aware of their daily activities and associations (Luthar, 2006; Luthar and Zelazo, 2003; Dishion and Kavanagh, 2003). Benson (1990) also found that such support can come from adults outside a child's family. Caring adults from outside a child's family may provide support for youth who have experienced unsatisfactory relationships within their families (Olds et al., 1997; Hawley and DeHaan, 1996; Werner and Smith, 1982, 1992).

GIRLS STUDY GROUP MEMBERS

Dr. Margaret A. Zahn, Principal Investigator, Girls Study Group (2004–March 2008) Senior Research Scientist, RTI International; Professor, North Carolina State University

Dr. Stephanie R. Hawkins, Principal Investigator, Girls Study Group (April 2008– Present) Research Clinical Psychologist, RTI International

Dr. Robert Agnew, Professor, Department of Sociology, Emory University

Dr. Elizabeth Cauffman, Assistant Professor, Department of Psychology and Social Behavior, University of California–Irvine

Dr. Meda Chesney-Lind, Professor, Women's Studies Program, University of Hawaii–Manoa

Dr. Gayle Dakof, Associate Research Professor, Department of Epidemiology and Public Health, University of Miami

Dr. Del Elliott, Director, Center for the Study and Prevention of Violence, University of Colorado

Dr. Barry Feld, Professor, School of Law, University of Minnesota

Dr. Diana Fishbein, Director, Transdisciplinary Behavioral Science Program, RTI International

Dr. Peggy Giordano, Professor of Sociology, Center for Family and Demographic Research, Bowling Green State University

Dr. Candace Kruttschnitt, Professor, Department of Sociology, University of Toronto

Dr. Jody Miller, Associate Professor, Department of Criminology and Criminal Justice, University of Missouri–St. Louis

Dr. Merry Morash, Professor, School of Criminal Justice, Michigan State University

Dr. Darrell Steffensmeier, Professor, Depart- ment of Sociology, Pennsylvania State University

Ms. Giovanna Taormina, Executive Director, Girls Circle Association

Dr. Donna-Marie Winn, Senior Research Scientist, Center for Social Demography and Ethnography, Duke University

School connectedness and success. Schools can play a significant role in protecting adolescents at risk for delinquency. The protective factors in schools include school connectedness (a positive perception of the school environment and positive interactions with people at school) and school success (measured by grade point average). School set-tings have the potential to provide an important and positive developmental context where students can excel socially and academically. School connectedness appears especially important to adolescents who experience adversity in their homes (Perkins and Jones, 2004) because school may be one of few contexts where such adolescents' achievements are recognized and celebrated (DHHS, 2001).

Success in school can also be a protective factor against delinquency. As noted above, Resnick and colleagues (2004) identified a good grade point average as the most salient protective factor distinguishing youth who do not engage in violence from those who do. Similarly, in a study of academic risk among inner-city adolescents, Ripple and Luthar (2000) found that success early in a student's academic career protected against negative outcomes such as delinquency later in adolescence.

Religiosity. The National Study of Youth and Religion found religious faith was important in the lives of many teens in the United States (Smith, 2005). Recent literature documents that religiosity, or how important religion is to someone, protects against many types of negative outcomes for adoles- cents, including delinquency (Ball, Armistead, and Austin, 2003; Bridges and Moore, 2002; Clark, 1995). However, some literature points to the limiting protective effect of religion, suggesting that religion only protects against minor offenses (Benda and Toombs, 2000; Burkett, 1993; Evans et al., 1995). Despite the lack of consensus in the field regarding the impact of religiosity on different types of delinquent behaviors, research has established that religion does, in fact, have some influence on some delinquent behaviors (Baier and Wright, 2001; Regnerus, 2003; Benda and Toombs, 2003; Evans et al., 1995).

Developmental Perspective

Protective factors may operate at different points during a child's development (Masten, Best, and Garmezy, 1990; Wright and Masten, 1997). When exploring the issue of resilience in youth, researchers must acknowledge that risk and protection occur within a normative developmental context (Spencer et al., 2006). An example of this sort of normative development is that the presence of a caring adult may protect a younger child from engaging in delinquent behaviors more than it would an older adolescent, the latter of whom is more developmentally influenced by peers than adults. Researchers should examine the protective factors that exist in a child's life and at what stage of a child's development they take effect. As children develop, their relationships with adults, the schools they attend, and the neighborhoods they live in increasingly affect their wellbeing and expose them to factors that protect them and to other factors that put them at risk for outcomes such as delinquency (Wright and Masten, 2005). Developmental transitions are important periods for observing resilience and the role of protective factors. Researchers lack information about how protective factors affect adolescent girls at varying levels of risk for delinquency and at different points in their development.

THE CURRENT STUDY

The study described in this Bulletin used data from the National Longitudinal Study of Adolescent Health (Add Health), to answer the following questions:

1. Do the presence of a caring adult, connection with and success in school, and religiosity protect girls from involvement in delinquent behaviors?
2. Do these protective factors operate differently for girls exposed to known risks for delinquency?

Although adolescent girls are exposed to myriad experiences that have the potential to increase their risk for delinquent behaviors, this Bulletin focuses on risks from personal victimization (physical abuse, sexual assault, and neglect) and structural barriers (neighborhood disadvantage). The largest proportion of delinquency cases involving girls occurred at age 15 (Snyder and Sickmund, 2006), when many of the negative experiences from childhood personal victimization and living in disadvantaged neighborhoods are already entrenched in their lives. To counteract these negative influences and develop interventions, researchers must examine the protective factors that can buffer girls from involvement in delinquency and determine which protective factors have the strength to overcome the impact of negative experiences childhood.

Data Source

The National Longitudinal Study of Adolescent Health used self-reported survey data to examine health-related behaviors in adolescence and subsequent outcomes in young adulthood (Udry, 2003). In two survey waves (1995 and 1996), Add Health researchers collected individual, family, school, and community-level information from a sample of approximately 19,000 students in grades 7–12 at 132 schools. In a third wave (2000–2001), approximately 15,000 of the original participants were resurveyed as young adults ages 18–26.

The analyses in this Bulletin are based on Add Health data for girls—9,641 in wave 1; 6,962 in wave 2; and 5,736 in wave 3. The benefit of using the Add Health survey data is that it can reveal which factors may protect the "average" adolescent girl, or a girl with known risk factors, from engaging in delinquent behavior. This is because longitudinal studies can identify typical patterns of development and reveal experiences or behaviors that impact a person's developmental trajectory. (For detailed information on the Add Health study, visit www.cpc.unc.edu/ projects/addhealth.)

Analyzing the Survey Data

Using data from the Add Health study, the authors created measures of risk and protective factors and delinquent/criminal outcomes.

Risk factors. The four risk indicators analyzed were physical assault by a parent or caregiver, sexual assault, neglect by a parent or caregiver, and neighborhood disadvantage.

- **Physical assault:** Being slapped, hit, or kicked more than 10 times by a parent/caregiver before the sixth grade (asked retrospectively in wave 3).

- **Sexual assault:** Forced sexual intercourse by any perpetrator during the previous 12 months (asked in wave 1); or any forced sexual contact, including intercourse or touching, with a parent or caregiver before the sixth grade (asked retrospectively in wave 3).

- **Neglect:** Being left alone when an adult should have been present more than 10 times before the sixth grade, or ever not having basic needs (such as food and clothing) met by the parent or caregiver before the sixth grade (asked retrospectively in wave 3).

- Neighborhood disadvantage: An index developed during wave 1, based on the percent of families living below poverty, percent of adults without a high school diploma or its equivalent, percent of female-headed households, and unemployment rate.

Protective factors. The four protective indicators were the presence of a caring adult, school connectedness, school success, and religiosity. The indicators were based on responses to questions in wave 1.

- **Caring adult:** Three questions about the degree to which respondents felt their parents, teachers, or other adults cared about them.

- **School connectedness:** Seven questions about respondents' perceptions of school and their interactions with peers and teachers.

- **School success:** GPA in math, science, social studies, language arts, and English.

- **Religiosity:** Three questions— frequency of praying and attending religious events and perceived importance of religion.

For the first three indicators, responses were averaged to create an overall measure. For religiosity, responses were standardized to a single response scale and averaged.

RESEARCH ON RISK FACTORS FOR DELINQUENCY

For girls, the key risk factors for delinquency and incarceration are family dysfunction, trauma and sexual abuse, mental health and substance abuse problems, high-risk sexual behaviors, school problems, and affiliation with deviant peers (Hubbard and Pratt, 2002; Lederman et al., 2004). Physical abuse and sexual abuse contribute to male and female involvement in delinquency (Dembo, Williams, and Schmeidler, 1993; Siegel and Senna, 2000), but female delinquents are more likely than their male counterparts to have been abused (Dembo, Williams, and Schmeidler, 1993). Researchers have also examined how conditions such as poverty and other forms of social and economic disadvantage can affect delinquent behaviors (Felner, 2005).

Delinquent and criminal outcomes. Delinquent and criminal outcomes were based on activities engaged in during adolescence (measured in wave 2) and/or late adolescence and young adulthood (measured in wave 3). These activities included status offenses (unexcused absence from school, unruliness in a public place); gang membership; selling drugs; committing a serious property offense (stealing something worth more than $50 or breaking and entering to steal something); and engaging in violence—simple assault (carrying a weapon or fighting with someone) or aggravated assault (using a weapon or seriously injuring someone).

FINDINGS

Table 1 shows the sample's racial and ethnic composition and summarizes risk factors and indicators of delinquent and criminal behavior. The majority of the female respondents were white (68 percent), followed by black respondents (16 percent) and Hispanic respondents (12 percent). During wave 1, nearly 6 percent of respondents reported being physically assaulted by their parent or caregiver more than 10 times before sixth grade, 10 percent reported being sexually assaulted, and nearly 9 percent reported being neglected by their parent or caregiver.

Table 1. Study Participants

	Unweighted Percent (Number) of Respondents		
	Wave 1 (*N*=9,641)	Wave 2 (*N*=6,963)	Wave 3 (*N*=5,736)
Race/ethnicity			
White	68 (6,556)	69 (4,804)	69 (3,958)
Black	16 (1,543)	15 (1,044)	15 (860)
Hispanic	12 (1,157)	12 (836)	11 (631)
Asian	2 (193)	2 (139)	3 (173)
American Indian	1 (96)	1 (70)	1 (57)
Other	1 (96)	1 (70)	1 (57)
Risk factors*			
Physical assault	5.5 (294)	—	—
Sexual assault	10.5 (518)	—	—
Neglect	8.9 (476)	—	—
Outcomes			
Serious property offense	—	5 (326)	6 (296)
Status offense	—	55 (3,309)	—
Simple assault	—	17 (1,036)	4 (209)
Aggravated assault	—	6 (410)	3 (189)
Gang membership	—	3 (194)	—
Selling drugs	—	4 (274)	—

* A fourth risk factor—disadvantaged neighborhood—was measured with four census-level socioeconomic indicators in wave 1 as a standardized score with mean of 0 and standard deviation of 0.866.

Protective factors and female delinquency. This analysis showed that—when controlling for general risk factor categories—the extent to which adolescent girls believed an adult cared about them served as a protective factor against several forms of delinquency (see table 2). During wave 1, girls who reported having more adults in their lives who cared about them were less likely to report committing status offenses, property offenses, selling drugs, gang mem-bership, simple assault, and aggravated assault during adolescence (wave 2) and less likely to report committing simple assault as young adults (wave 3).

Table 2. Effects of Protective Factors on Delinquent or Criminal Behavior

Protective Factor (wave 1)	Behaviors									
	Status Offense (wave 2)	Gang Membership (wave 2)	Selling Drugs (wave 2)	Property Offense (wave 2)	Property Offense (wave 3)	Simple Assault (wave 2)	Simple Assault (wave 3)	Aggravated Assault (wave 2)	Aggravated Assault (wave 3)
School Success	Protective 0.76 (0.67, 0.85)	Protective 0.47 (0.33, 0.67)	NS	Protective 0.62 (0.45, 0.85)	Risk Enhan-cing 1.25 (1.03, 1.51)	Protective 0.54 (0.47, 0.63)	Protective 0.58 (0.45, 0.75)	Protective 0.57 (0.47, 0.70)	Protective 0.58 (0.40, 0.83)
Caring Adult	Protective (0.55 (0.46, 0.65)	Protective 0.66 (0.45, 0.98)	Protective 0.61 (0.45, 81)	Protective 0.63 (0.48, 82)	NS	Protective 0.71 (0.59, 0.86)	Protective 0.58 (0.41, 0.80)	Protective 0.64 (0.48, 0.85)	NS
School Connec-tedness	NS	NS	NS	NS	NS	NS	NS	NS	Risk Enha-ncing 1.98 (1.11, 3.54)
Religiosity	NS	NS	Protective 0.76 (0.63, 0.92)	NS	NS	NS	NS	NS	NS

Note: The table shows the results of logistic regression analysis. Protective = A statistically significant protective effect against the behavior. The extent of the effect is indicated by the numbers in the table (odds ratios); odds ratios greater than 1 indicate greater likelihood of the criminal/delinquent behavior, odds ratios less than 1 indicate the behavior is less likely. The confidence interval for the odds ratios (a measure of their precision) is 95 percent. NS = The protective effect was not statistically significant, or there was no protective effect.

Contrary to the findings of previous research, school connectedness did not serve as a protective factor in this study. In fact, girls who reported higher levels of school connectedness in wave 1 were more likely to report being involved in aggravated assault by young adulthood.

School success was a significant protective factor during adolescence (wave 2) and young adulthood (wave 3) for some forms of delinquent behaviors. Adolescent girls who reported greater school success during the initial data collection were less likely to report status offenses and gang membership 1 year later (wave 2) and less likely to report simple assault and aggravated assault during late adolescence and young adulthood (wave 3). However, girls who were successful in school were more likely to commit a property offense during late adolescence and young adulthood.

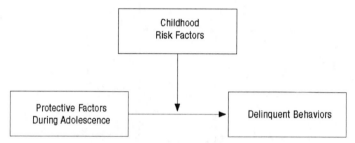

During adolescence, some girls have protective experiences in their lives that assist them in being resilient from engaging in delinquent and criminal behaviors. However, some protective factors may not be strong enough to mitigate the influence of risk factors that may have endured since childhood. The interaction between these risk and protective factors can decrease, attenuate, or increase a girl's propensity towards delinquent behavior.

Figure 1. Interaction of Childhood Risk Factors and Protective Factors in Adolescence

Religiosity did not serve as a protective factor against delinquent behaviors, with one exception: girls reporting higher levels of religiosity in wave 1 reported lower incidents of selling drugs in wave 2.

Interactions of risk and protective factors. Table 2 does not take into account the girls' specific likelihood of risk for delinquency as measured by the risk factors listed in table 1. To better understand the nature of resilience, the authors explored the effects of childhood risk factors on the interaction between the protective factors girls experienced during early adolescence and their subsequent delinquent or criminal behaviors in mid-adolescence and late adolescence/early adulthood. This model is depicted in figure 1. Table 3 (pg. 7) shows the results of this analysis.

A risk factor can modify the effects of protective factors in three ways:

1. By enhancing the protective effect (i.e., the benefits of the protective effect keep a problem behavior from occurring).
2. By attenuating the protective effect (i.e., weakening the benefi-cial effect).
3. By negating the beneficial effect or by changing the direction of the effect (i.e., the protective effect in the general population is not protective in the at-risk population or is associated with increased negative behavior).

Results showed that risk factors modified the effects of protective factors in the following ways:

Although the presence of a caring n adult reduced the likelihood that girls would sell drugs whether or not they lived in a disadvantaged neighborhood, this protective effect was weakened in severely disadvantaged neighborhoods.

- For property offenses, gang membership, and aggravated assault, the risk factor of physical assault enhanced the protective effect provided by a caring adult. The rates of these behaviors among girls who reported having caring adults in their lives decreased more sharply from wave 2 to wave 3 for girls who had been physically assaulted than for those who had not.
- Not every finding supports the premise that a caring adult was protective against engaging in delinquent behavior when a girl is exposed to risk situations. For example, girls who had been physically assaulted were more likely to report engaging in aggravated assault

during late adolescence or early adulthood (wave 3) if they had a caring adult in their lives. Similarly, girls who reported being neglected were more likely to join a gang during adolescence if they also reported having caring adults in their lives.

- School success protected against involvement in aggravated assault among girls from disadvantaged neighborhoods, but the protection decreased as the level of neighborhood disadvantage increased. Although school success protected adolescent girls from simple assault in the general population, sexually assaulted girls were more likely to engage in simple assault during adolescence if they were successful in school. The protective effect of school connectedness against involvement in simple assault during late adolescence or early adulthood (wave 3) was greater among girls who had been physically assaulted.
- Religiosity protected girls in late adolescence or early adulthood from involvement in:
  - Simple assault—if they came from disadvantaged neighborhoods.
  - Aggravated assault—if they had been sexually assaulted.

However, religiosity was associated with increased likelihood of:

- Aggravated assault during late adolescence or early adulthood—if the girls had been physically assaulted.
- Gang membership during adolescence—if the girls had been neglected.

STUDY LIMITATIONS

The potential inaccuracy of retrospective self-reported data in assessing delinquent behaviors is a limitation in this investigation. Schroeder and colleagues (2003) found that people tend to overreport situations that they view as significant, even if these events do not occur frequently. However, people may forget or underreport events that they view as minor or insignificant even if these events occur frequently. This suggests that youth participating in the Add Health study who engaged in delinquent behaviors over an extended period of time or who had been physically or sexually abused or neglected may have given less accurate self-reports, depending on the duration and perceived importance of the events they were reporting.

Table 3. How Childhood Risk Factors and Protective Factors in Adolescence[1] Interact to Produce or Prevent Delinquent Behavior

Risk Factor	Delinquent Behavior						
	Status offense	Gang Membership	Selling Drugs	Property Offense	Simple Assault	Aggravated Assault
If a girl was physically assaulted as a child...				...**the presence of a caring adult reduced the** likelihood that she would become involved in property crime in adolescence.[2]	...**school connectedness** reduced the likelihood that she would commit simple assault in young adulthood.[2]	...**the presence of a caring adult reduced the likelihood that she would commit aggravated assault in adolescence**.[2] ...**religiosity and the presence of a caring adult** increased the likelihood that she would commit aggravated assault in young adulthood.[3]
If a girl was sexually assaulted as a child...					...**school success** reduced the likelihood that she would commit simple assault in adolescence.[2]	...religiosity reduced the likelihood that she would commit aggravated assault in young adulthood.[2]
If a girl spent her childhood in a disadvantaged neighborhood...			...**the presence of a caring adult** minimally reduced the likelihood that she would sell drugs in adolescence.[2]		...religiosity reduced the likelihood that she would commit simple assault in young adulthood.[2]	...school success minimally reduced the likelihood that she would commit aggravated assault in adolescence.[2]

Table 3. (Continued)

Risk Factor	Status offense	Gang Membership	Selling Drugs	Property Offense	Simple Assault	Aggravated Assault
			Delinquent Behavior			
If a girl was neglected as a child...		...religiosity and the presence of a caring adult increased the likelihood that she would join a gang in adolescence.[3]				

[1] All protective factors—a caring adult, school connectedness, school success, and religiosity—occurred during a girl's adolescence.

[2] The protective factor had a greater effect for girls who had not been exposed to this risk factor. In some circumstances, protective factors stabilized the risk of delinquent behavior, making it equivalent to that of girls who had not experienced a risk factor, rather than protecting risk-exposed girls more than their counterparts.

[3] These factors protected girls who had not been exposed to this risk factor.

The Add Health questions that focused on abuse and neglect required youth to recall the number of times particular events occurred and interpret whether or not certain behaviors were acceptable. However, such youth may have difficulty judging when they are being abused or neglected. Hardt and Rutter (2004) found that youth often have difficulty recalling experiences that rely primarily on this type of judgment, which suggests that the prevalence of these behaviors may be underrepresented.

The desire to avoid shame and embarrassment by conforming to perceived social norms (i.e., social desirability) is another limitation in the accuracy of self-report assessments. Although the Add Health study design attempted to reduce this type of inaccuracy by asking sensitive questions via Audio Computer-Assisted Self Interviewing (ACASI), this may not have eliminated social desirability effects.

Another limitation is that Add Health findings cannot be generalized to girls who are deeply involved in the juvenile justice system. Because Add Health surveyed a nationally representative sample of adolescents, these data can reveal which factors protect the average adolescent girl from engaging in delinquent behaviors but do not provide an accurate view of risk and protective factors in the lives of girls with extensive delinquent histories.

The final limitations include using grade point average as the sole measure of school success and the fact that all of the questions used to measure risk factors in this study provided data on childhood risks (occurring either before sixth grade or at a time before the first data collection), and did not account for risks encountered later in life. This limited the possibility of exploring how protective factors affected girls who may have only encountered risks after childhood.

IMPLICATIONS

The most consistent protective effect assessed in this study was the extent to which a girl felt she had caring adults in her life. The presence of caring adults reduced the likelihood that girls would engage in several forms of delinquent behaviors; however, this protective effect was not consistent for girls at high risk for delinquency. Physically assaulted girls were protected when they believed they had a caring adult in their lives during mid-adolescence but not in young adulthood. They were less likely to report property offenses and engage in aggravated assault as adolescents than girls who had not been physically assaulted, but reported engaging in more aggravated assault as they moved into young adulthood.

These findings are contrary to previous findings and to the general expectation that caring adults provide a form of protection (Dishion and Kavanagh, 2003; Romer, 2003; Benson, 1990; Hawley and DeHaan, 1996; Werner and Smith, 1982, 1992). Research conducted by Perkins and Jones (2004) on the risk behaviors among physically abused adolescents concluded that adolescents who seek adults outside of their family for support may do so because of the perceived inability to obtain the support they need from their parents. The girls in this investigation who were physically assaulted and have moved into early adulthood may have decided that the adults in their lives have failed them. Moreover, they may have found support from other adults who were not good role models for prosocial behavior.

School connectedness protected physically assaulted girls from engaging in delinquent behaviors. When physically assaulted girls felt connected to their schools, they were less likely to report committing simple assault than girls who had not been assaulted. School, for physically assaulted girls, may provide a refuge from an unsafe home environment. Because the majority of a youth's day is spent at school, becoming connected with this institution and the resources available therein seems to serve as a protection against delinquency for physically assaulted girls.

School success, as measured by having a high grade point average, did not protect physically assaulted girls from delinquency. School success served as a significant protection against several forms of delinquency for girls in the general population and helped girls in disadvantaged neighborhoods refrain from delinquent behavior. During early adolescence, having a higher GPA made it less likely that girls would engage in delinquency (status offenses, property crimes, gang membership, simple assault, and aggravated assault) with the exception of selling drugs, which was not significant. During early adulthood, a high GPA no longer protected against engaging in property crimes, and in fact, was associated with an increased likelihood of engaging in this behavior.

School success was less protective for girls who had been sexually or physically abused or lived in disadvantaged neighborhoods. Girls who had been sexually abused and had high GPAs were more likely to engage in simple assault in mid-adolescence. Although having a high GPA served as a protective factor against aggravated assault, this protection weakened with increased neighborhood disadvantage. Other studies have also demonstrated that academic competence may not have positive consequences for economically disadvantaged adolescents living in high-risk environments (Luthar, 1999; Luthar, Cicchetti, and Becker, 2000; Luthar, Doernberger, and Zigler, 1993). As neighborhood disadvantage increases, girls may encounter situations that make violence a more useful coping behavior in the short term than focusing on school success, whose benefit is not revealed immediately. Additionally, girls from disadvantaged neighborhoods likely attend disadvantaged schools. School success may not lead to the same beneficial outcomes as that experienced by girls in more advantaged schools and neighborhoods.

According to Steinman (2005), youth at different risk levels for delinquency may sell drugs. Religiosity helped protect girls who were not at high risk for delinquency from selling drugs during early adolescence.

Muller and Ellison (2001) found that religion can have different effects for girls at differing levels of risk for delinquency. In this study, religiosity helped protect girls who were not a high risk for delinquency against nonviolent delinquent behaviors. Religiosity also helped protect girls at high risk for delinquency from violent behavior.

The types of risk encountered during childhood influence whether religiosity will have a protective effect on girls' delinquent behavior. Girls from disadvantaged neighborhoods and those who had been sexually abused were less likely to engage in violent forms of delinquency when they were religious. However, girls who had been neglected or physically assaulted were more likely to engage in aggravated assault when they were religious.

The work of Brody and colleagues (1996) provides some explanation for this finding. Their work found religiosity "gives rise to a belief system that produces norms that are directly and indirectly linked to youth competence." The finding suggests that when girls are neglected and experience repeated physical assault early in life, their belief systems may become skewed to support the idea that violence is an acceptable and normal behavior. Additionally, if girls who are physically abused live in homes where religious beliefs are promoted, religion could function as a belief system that supports violence.

CONCLUSION

Abuse, neglect, poverty, and violence threaten the development and behavior of many youth, yet some remain resilient. The factors underlying female resilience are still being discovered. Participation in delinquent acts is not limited to girls whose circumstances place them at high risk for delinquency. The results of this study suggest that the presence of a caring adult, school success, school connectedness, and religiosity may protect against some forms of delinquent behavior for girls, but this protective effect is subject to complex interactions with risk factors and age. Understanding the role these protective factors play in the lives of girls has important implications for creating programs to prevent delinquency.

A concerted attention to context is needed when developing interventions designed to promote resilience (Luthar, 2006). Although some of the factors examined in this study protected girls from engaging in delinquent behaviors, many of these protective factors had a differential effect in girls who faced severe adversity—including physical and sexual assault, neglect, and neighborhood disadvantage. These findings highlight the importance of considering the life histories and stressors that are present when developing interventions for girls at high risk for delinquency. Interventions that help adolescent girls learn how to manage their risk (e.g., effectively dealing with the trauma of childhood physical and sexual assault) would be an important contribution to the delinquency prevention field (Ruffolo, Sarri, and Goodkind, 2004). Additionally, interventions should focus on the protective factors that mitigate risk (Luthar, 2006). According to researcher Ann Masten, the ability to match the tasks and activities of a particular intervention program to those factors that protect program participants from negative outcomes may be the single most important contribution resilience research can make to delinquency program development (Masten, 1994).

For some girls exposed to childhood risks, caring adults, school connectedness, school success, and religiosity helped to prevent certain forms of delinquency during early adolescence, but in other cases, these protective factors were not strong enough to mitigate the impact of the risks. This underscores the notion that one delinquency prevention program cannot be tailored to the needs of all girls who are at risk for delinquency.

As a first step, researchers must understand how protective factors operate in girls' lives and when these protective factors are most relevant to girls' development. Secondly, researchers should understand the risks confronting adolescent girls and consider which protective factors are strong enough to mitigate particular risks. Future empirically-based effectiveness studies on delinquency prevention may provide the field with more evidence of factors that protect girls from delinquent behavior.

REFERENCES

Acoca, L. (1999). Investing in girls: A 21st century strategy. *Juvenile Justice, 6,* 2-21.

Baier, C. & Wright, B. R. E. (2001). "If you love me, keep my commandments": A meta-analysis of the effect of religion on crime. *Journal of Research on Crime and Delinquency, 38(1),* 3-21.

Ball, J., Armistead, L. & Austin, B. (2003). The relationship between religiosity and adjustment among African American, female, urban adolescents. *Journal of Adolescence, 26,* 431-446.

Benda, B. B. & Toombs, N. J. (2000). Religiosity and violence—Are they related after considering the strongest predictors? *Journal of Criminal Justice, 28,* 483-496.

Benson, P. L. (1990). *The Troubled Journey: A Portrait of 6th–12th Grade Youth.* Minneapolis, MN: Search Institute.

Bridges, L. J. & Moore, K. A. (2002). Religious involvement and children's well-being: What research tells us (and what it doesn't). Child Trends Research Brief. Washington, DC: Child Trends.

Brody, G. H., Stoneman, Z. & Flor, D. (1996). Parental religiosity, family processes, and youth competence in rural, two-parent African American families. *Developmental Psychology, 32,* 696-706.

Burkett, S. R. (1993). Perceived parents' religiosity, friends' drinking, and hellfire: A panel study of adolescent drinking. *Review of Religious Research, 35,* 136-154.

Clark, P. (1995). *Risk and resilience in adolescence: The current status of research on gender differences (Equity Issues, No. 1).* Columbus, OH: The Ohio State University, Department of Home Economics Education.

Dembo, R., Williams, L. & Schmeidler, J. (1993). Gender differences in mental health service needs among youths entering a juvenile detention center. *Journal of Prison and Jail Health, 12,* 73-101.

Dishion, T. J. & Kavanagh, K. (2003). *Intervening in Adolescent Prob-lem Behavior: A Family-Centered Approach.* New York: Guilford Press.

Doll, B. & Lyon, M. A. (1998). Risk and resilience: Implications for the delivery of educational and mental health services in schools. *School Psychology Review, 27,* 348-363.

Evans, D. T., Cullen, F. T., Dunaway, R. G. & Burton, V. S. (1995). Religion and crime reexamined: The impact of religion, secular controls, and social ecology on adult criminality. *Criminology, 33,* 195-217.

Felner, R. (2005). Poverty in childhood and adolescence. In *Handbook of Resilience in Children,* edited by S. Goldstein, & R. Brook,s. Kluwer Academic/Plenum Publishers: New York.

Fraser, M., Kirby, L. D. & Smokowski, P. R. (2004). Risk and resilience in childhood. In *Risk and Resilience in Childhood: An Ecological Perspective,* 2nd ed., edited by M. Fraser. Washington, DC: NASW Press.

Hardt, J. & Rutter, M. (2004). Validity of adult retrospective reports of adverse childhood experienes: Review of the evidence. *Journal of Child Psychology and Psychiatry, 45(2),* 260-273.

Hawley, D. R. & DeHaan, L. (1996). Toward a definition of family resilience: Integrating life-span and family perspectives. *Family Process, 35,* 283-298.

Herrenkohl, T. I., Tajima, E. A., Whitney, S. D. & Huang, B. (2005). Protection against antisocial behavior in children exposed to physically abusive discipline. *Journal of Adolescent Health, 36,* 457-465.

Hubbard, D. J. & Pratt, T. C. (2002). A meta-analysis of the predictors of delinquency among girls. *Journal of Offender Rehabilitation, 34,* 1-13.

Kaplan, H. B. (2005). Understanding the concept of resilience. In *Handbook of Resilience in Children,* edited by S. Goldstein and R. Brooks. New York, NY: Kluwer Academic/Plenum Publishers, 39-47.

Lederman, C. S., Dakof, G. A., Larrea, M. A. & Li, H. (2004). Characteristics of adolescent females in juvenile detention. *International Journal of Law and Psychiatry, 27*, 321-337.

Luthar, S. S. (1999). *Poverty and Children's Adjustment.* Thousand Oaks, CA: Sage Publications, Inc.

Luthar, S. S. (2006). Resilience in development: A synthesis of research across five decades. In *Developmental Psychopathology, Vol. 3: Risk, Disorder, and Adaptation* (2nd ed.), edited by S. D. Cicchetti, & D. J. Cohen, Hoboken, NJ: John Wiley and Sons, Inc., 739-795.

Luthar, S. S., Cicchetti, D. & Becker, B. (2000). The construct of resilience: A critical evaluation and guidelines for future work. *Child Development, 71*, 543-562.

Luthar, S. S., Doernberger, C. H. & Zigler, E. (1993). Resilience is not a unidimensional construct: Insights from a prospective study of inner-city adolescents. *Development and Psychopathology, 5*, 703-717. (Special Issue: Milestones in the development of resilience).

Luthar, S. S. & Zelazo, L. B. (2003). Research on resilience: An integrative review. In *Resilience and VulnerAbility: Adaptation in the Context of Childhood Adversities,* edited by S. S. Luthar, New York: Cambridge, *5*, 10-549.

Masten, A. (1994). Resilience in individual development: Successful adaptation despite risk and adversity. In *Risk and Resilience in Inner City America: Challenges and Prospects,* edited by M. Wang, & E. Gordon, Hillsdale, NJ: Erlbaum, 3-25.

Masten, A. S., Best, K. M. & Garmezy, N. (1990). Resilience and development: Contributions from the study of children who overcome adversity. *Development and Psychopathology, 2*, 425-444.

McKnight, L. R. & Loper, A. B. (2002). The effect of risk and resilience factors on the prediction of delinquency in adolescent girls. *School Psychology International, 23(2)*, 186-198.

Muller, C. & Ellison, C. (2001). Religious involvement, social capital, and adolescents' academic progress: Evidence from the National Education Longitudinal Study of 1988. *Sociological Focus, 34(2)*, 155-183.

Olds, D., Kitzman, H., Cole, R. & Robinson, J. (1997). Theoretical foundations of a program of home visitation for pregnant women and parents of young children. *Journal of Community Psychology, 25*, 9-25.

Olsson, C. A., Bond, L. & Burns, J. M. (2003). Adolescent resilence: A concept analysis. *Journal of Adolescence, 26(1)*, 1-11.

Perkins, D. F. & Jones, K. R. (2004). Risk behaviors and resiliency within physically abused adolescents. *Child Abuse and Neglect, 28,* 547-563.

Regnerus, M. D. (2003). Linked lives, faith, and behavior: Intergenerational religious influence on adolescent delinquency. *Journal for the Scientific Study of Religion, 42(2),* 189-203.

Resnick, M. D., Bearman, P. S. & Blum, R. W., et al. (1997). Protecting adolescents from harm: Findings from the National Longitudinal Study on Adolescent Health. *Journal of the American Medical Association, 278(10),* 823-832.

Resnick, M. S., Ireland, M. & Borowsky, I. (2004). Youth violence perpetration: What protects? What predicts? Findings from the National Longitudinal Study of Adolescent Health. *Journal of Adolescent Health, 35(5),* 424e1-424e10.

Ripple, C. H. & Luthar, S. (2000). Academic risk among inner-city adolescents: The role of personal attributes. *Journal of School Psychology, 38 (3),* 277-298.

Romer, D. (2003). *Reducing Adolescent Risk: Toward an Integrated Approach.* Thousand Oaks, CA: Sage Publications, Inc.

Ruffolo, M. C., Sarri, R. & Good- kind, S. (2004). Study of delinquent, diverted, and high-risk adolescent girls: Implications for mental health intervention. *Social Work Research, 28(4),* 237-245.

Schroeder, K. E., Carey, M. P. & Vanable, P. A. (2003). Methodological challenges in research on sexual risk behavior, II: Accuracy of self-reports. *Annals of Behavioral Medicine, 26(2),* 104-123.

Siegel, L. J. & Senna, J. J. (2000). *Juvenile Delinquency: Theory, Practice, and Law* (7th ed.). Belmont, CA: Wadsworth.

Smith, C. (2005). *Soul Searching: The Religious and Spiritual Lives of American Teenagers.* New York, NY: Oxford University Press.

Smith, C., Faris, R., Denton, M. L. & Regnerus, M. (2003). Mapping American adolescent subjective religiosity and attitudes of alienation toward religion: A research report. *Sociology of Religion, 64,* 111-133.

Smokowski, P. R. (1998). Prevention and intervention strategies for promoting resilience in disadvantaged children. *Social Service Review, 72(3),* 337-364.

Snyder, H. N. & Sickmund, M. (2006). *Juvenile Offenders and Victims: 2006 National Report.* Washington, DC: U.S. Department of Justice, Office of Justice Programs, Office of Juvenile Justice and Delinquency Prevention.

Spencer, M. B., Harpalani, V., Cassidy, E., Jacobs, C. Y., Donde, S., Goss, T. N., Munoz-Miller, M., Charles, N. & Wilson, S. (2006). Understanding vulnerability and resilience from a normative developmental perspective: Implications for racially and ethnically diverse youth. In *Developmental Psychopathology—Volume 1: Theory and Method,* edited by D. Cicchetti, & D. J. Cohen, New Jersey: John Wiley and Sons.

Steinman, K. J. (2005). Drug selling among high school students: Related risk behaviors and psychosocial characteristics. *Journal of Adolescent Health, 36,* 71e1-71e8.

Udry, J. R. (2003). The National Longitudinal Study of Adolescent Health. *Paper presented at the annual meeting of the American Sociological Association,* Atlanta, GA, August 16.

U.S. Department of Health and Human Services. (2001). *Youth Violence: A Report of the Surgeon General.* Rockville, MD: U.S. Department of Health and Human Services, Centers for Disease Control and Prevention, National Center for Injury Prevention and Control; Substance Abuse and Mental Health Services Administration, Center for Mental Health Services; and National Institutes of Health, National Institute of Mental Health.

Werner, E. (2005). What can we learn about resilience from large-scale longitudinal studies? In *Handbook of Resilience in Children,* edited by S. Goldstein and R. Brooks. New York, NY: *Kluwer Academic/Plenum Publishers, 9 ,* 1-105.

Werner, E. & Smith, R. (1982). *Vulnerable, not Invincible: A Longitudinal Study of Resilient Children and Youth.* New York: McGraw–Hill.

Werner, E. & Smith, R. (1992). *Overcoming the Odds: High Risk Children From Birth to Adulthood.* Ithaca, NY: Cornell University.

Wright, M. O. & Masten, A. S. (1997). Vulnerability and resilience in young children. In Handbook of Child and Adolescent Psychiatry: Vol. 1, Infancy and Preschoolers: Development and Syndromes, edited by J. D., Noshpitz, S., Greenspan, S. Wieder, & J. Osof- sky. New York: Wiley, 202-224.

Wright, M. O. & Masten, A. S. (2005). Resilience process in develop-ment. In Handbook of Resilience in Children, edited by S. Goldstein, & R. Brooks, New York: Kluwer Academ-ic 17-37.

Yates, T., Egeland, B. & Sroufe, L. (2003). Rethinking resilience: A devel-opmental process perspective. In Resilience and Vulnerability: *Adap-tation in the Context of Childhood Adversities*, edited by S. S. Luthar, New York: Cambridge, 243-266.

ACKNOWLEDGMENTS

Stephanie R. Hawkins, Ph.D., is a Research Clinical Psychologist in the Crime, Violence, and Justice Research Program at RTI International.

Phillip W. Graham, DrPH, is a Senior Public Health Researcher in the Crime, Violence, and Justice Research Program at RTI International.

Jason Williams, Ph.D., is a Research Psychologist in the Risk Behavior and Family Research Program at RTI International.

Margaret A. Zahn, Ph.D., was a Principal Scientist at RTI International and a professor at North Carolina State University during her Girls Study Group directorship, and is currently Acting Deputy Director of Research and Evaluation at the National Institute of Justice.

This Bulletin was prepared under cooperative agreement number #2004–JF–FX–K001 from the Office of Juvenile Justice and Delinquency Prevention (OJJDP), U.S. Department of Justice.

Points of view or opinions expressed in this document are those of the author(s) and do not necessarily represent the official position or policies of OJJDP or the U.S. Department of Justice.

In: Not So Nice: Girls' Delinquency Issues   ISBN: 978-1-60876-268-2
Editor: Adam P. Mawer   © 2010 Nova Science Publishers, Inc.

Chapter 5

VIOLENCE BY TEENAGE GIRLS: TRENDS AND CONTEXT[*]

Margaret A. Zahn, Susan Brumbaugh,
Darrell Steffensmeier, Barry C. Feld, Merry Morash,
Meda Chesney-Lind, Jody Miller, Allison Ann Payne,
Denise C. Gottfredso and Candace Kruttschnitt

According to data from the Federal Bureau of Investigation, from 1991 to 2000, arrests of girls increased more (or decreased less) than arrests of boys for most types of offenses. By 2004, girls accounted for 30 percent of all juvenile arrests. However, questions remain about whether these trends reflect an actual increase in girls' delinquency or changes in societal responses to girls' behavior. To find answers to these questions, the Office of Juvenile Justice and Delinquency Prevention (OJJDP) convened the Girls Study Group to establish a theoretical and empirical foundation to guide the development, testing, and dissemination of strategies to reduce or prevent girls' involvement in delinquency and violence.

The Girls Study Group Series, of which this Bulletin is a part, presents the Group's findings. The series examines issues such as patterns of offending among adolescents and how they differ for girls and boys; risk

---

[*] This is an edited, reformatted and augmented version of a U. S. Department of Justice publication dated May 2008.

and protective factors associated with delinquency, including gender differences; and the causes and correlates of girls' delinquency.

In June 2005, *Newsweek* ran a story titled "Bad Girls Go Wild," which described "the significant rise in violent behavior among girls" as a "burgeoning national crisis" (Scelfo, 2005)—a depiction that echoes other recent media accounts. This Bulletin assesses the accuracy of these assertions using the best available data. Drawing on information from official arrest sources, nationally based self-report and victimization surveys, and studies reported in the social science literature, the Bulletin examines the involvement of girls in violent activity (including whether such activity has increased relative to the increase for boys) and the contexts in which girls engage in violent behavior.

One of the most consistent and robust findings in criminology is that, for nearly every offense, females engage in much less crime and juvenile delin quency than males. In recent years, however, the extent and character of this gender difference in offending are increasingly being called into ques tion by statistics and media reports suggesting the increasing involvement of girls in the juvenile and criminal justice systems. During the past two and-a-half decades, official statistics suggest that female delinquency has undergone substantial changes compared with male delinquency. Between 1980 and 2005, arrests of girls increased nationwide, while arrests of boys decreased (Federal Bureau of Investigation, 2006). These arrest trends, along with high-profile cases of female delinquency, have become the main support for media headlines.

However, because arrest counts are a product of both delinquent behavior and official responses to it, researchers and policymakers face a dilemma about how to interpret the arrest statistics. Do the increases in arrests indicate real changes in girls' behaviors, or are the increases a product of recent changes in public sentiment and enforcement policies that have elevated the visibility and reporting of girls' delinquency and violence? This Bulletin attempts to answer this question.

TRENDS IN GIRLS' VIOLENCE

This Bulletin relies on three data sources—official arrest data, self- report data, and victimization data— to examine trends in girls' violence from 1980 through 2005. Each source has strengths and weaknesses and provides a somewhat different pic ture of crime.

Data Sources

Official sources of data on delinquency include information collected and disseminated by local agencies such as police, as well as State and national organizations that disseminate information collected at the local level. The primary source of official data on delinquency comes from the Federal Bureau of Investigation's (FBI's) Uniform Crime Report (UCR), published annually. Each UCR reflects thousands of local police reports on crimes known to police and on arrests, from which the FBI compiles statistics on the type of crime (roughly 30 broad categories), the location of the arrest (urban, sub urban, or rural), and the demograph ic characteristics of the offender (e.g., age, gender).

GIRLS STUDY GROUP MEMBERS

Dr. Margaret Zahn, Senior Research Scientist, RTI International; Professor, North Carolina State University

Dr. Robert Agnew, Professor, Department of Sociology, Emory University

Dr. Elizabeth Cauffman, Assistant Professor, Department of Psychology and Social Behavior, University of California, Irvine

Dr. Meda Chesney-Lind, Professor, Women's Studies Program, University of Hawaii at Manoa

Dr. Gayle Dakof, Associate Research Professor, Department of Epidemiology and Public Health, University of Miami

Dr. Del Elliott, Director, Center for the Study and Prevention of Violence, University of Colorado

Dr. Barry Feld, Professor, School of Law, University of Minnesota

Dr. Diana Fishbein, Director, Transdisciplinary Behavioral Science Program, RTI International

Dr. Peggy Giordano, Professor of Sociology, Center for Family and Demographic Research, Bowling Green State University

Dr. Candace Kruttschnitt, Professor, Department of Sociology, University of Minnesota

Dr. Jody Miller, Associate Professor, Department of Criminology and Criminal Justice, University of Missouri–St. Louis

Dr. Merry Morash, Professor, School of Criminal Justice, Michigan State University

Dr. Darrell Steffensmeier, Professor, Department of Sociology, Pennsylvania State University

Ms. Giovanna Taormina, Executive Director, Girls Circle Association

Dr. Donna-Marie Winn, Senior Research Scientist, Center for Child and Family Policy, Duke University

---

VIOLENCE DEFINED

Many different sources of data examine violence and girls' involvement in it. However, these sources often rely on different definitions and measures of violence. Official criminal justice system data sources (e.g., Uniform Crime Reports) use legal definitions focusing on homicide, rape, robbery, aggravated assault (which usually involves assault with a weapon or assault producing injury), and simple assault (a behavior defined differently in various jurisdictions). Self-report studies and those involving interviews with adolescents focus on a variety of behaviors including, for example, fighting and weapon-carrying. Some studies include relational aggression in their definitions of violent behavior (see p. 11 for a discussion of relational aggression). In general, this Bulletin defines violence as behaviors that inflict or threaten to inflict bodily injury on other persons.

Self-report surveys on juvenile crime and its correlates are another major source of information. In addition to the detailed information on respondent characteristics, the main benefit of self-report data is the information obtained on crimes that were committed by youth but not known to the police. Most self-report delinquency surveys are cross-sectional (i.e., cover only one point in time) and localized (i.e., limited to a particular community or region). Among the surveys that provide longitudinal or trend data on youth delinquency for the Nation as a whole, the authors use Monitoring the Future (MTF).[1] MTF is an ongoing study of the behaviors, attitudes, and values of American secondary school students. Each year, a total of approximately 50,000 8th, 10th, and 12th grade students are surveyed (12th graders since 1975, and 8th and 10th graders since 1991).

Victimization surveys provide a third important source of information on delinquent behavior. These types of data provide a different perspective. Whereas information on self-reported delinquent activity is collected from the offender, the source of infor mation for victimization surveys is the victim of criminal activity. The Census Bureau has conducted the National Crime Victimization Sur vey (NCVS) for the Bureau of Justice Statistics annually since 1973. Each year, NCVS interviews individuals age 12 and older in a nationally representative sample of approximately 50,000 households. Victims of various types of crimes (including violent and property crimes) report detailed characteristics of criminal events, including time and location, level of physical and property damage, and—in the case of violent crime—the perceived characteristics (e.g., age, gender, race) of the offender(s).

PRIMARY DATA SOURCES

- Uniform Crime Reports (UCR) arrest data.
- Monitoring the Future (MTF).
- National Crime Victimization Survey (NCVS).

TRENDS IN ARRESTS FOR VIOLENT OFFENSES: UCR DATA

In 2005, out of 14 million arrests, 2.1 million involved juveniles (Snyder, forthcoming).[2] Juveniles comprised about 15 percent of arrests for all offenses, about 16 percent of arrests for Violent Crime Index[3] offenses, and about 26 percent of arrests for Property Crime Index[4] offenses. Girls comprised nearly one-third (29 per cent) of all juvenile arrests, about one-third (34 percent) of arrests for Property Crime Index offenses, and less than one-fifth (18 percent) of arrests for Violent Crime Index offenses. Although serious and vio lent crimes capture media and public attention, the vast majority of juve nile arrests are for less serious offens es—nonindex and status offenses[5] accounted for three-quarters (76 per cent) of all juvenile arrests.

LIMITATIONS

All three data sources have limitations. The official or arrest data capture only detected offenses—those that are known to the police or that result in an arrest. Reporting police agencies also vary widely in their reporting coverage. Some jurisdictions have 100-percent reporting, while other jurisdictions are underrepresented. Moreover, because offense categories are very broad, conclusions may be misleading.[*] For example, the increase in girls' arrests for "serious crimes" (i.e., UCR Index Crimes, as discussed and defined later in this Bulletin) is largely attributable to the inclusion of larceny-theft in that category. Furthermore, arrest data may be affected by changes in enforcement policy that may affect one gender more than the other. Given the gender difference in the character and context of delinquency (i.e., that girls generally engage in less serious forms of crime), changes in laws and enforcement toward targeting less serious forms of lawbreaking may disproportionately impact the risk of arrest for females.

Limitations of self-report and victimization data are that they typically cover only a few forms of lawbreaking and have sampling deficiencies (e.g., MTF is administered in schools and so would underreport crimes committed by youth who have dropped out of school or are frequently truant, and NCVS only interviews victims who are age 12 and older). These data are, however, particularly useful for thinking about whether girls' delinquency trends reflect changes in underlying behavior or changes in enforcement and arrest policies—at least when data sources overlap for the forms of law-violating behavior being measured. For example, longitudinal arrest data on assault can be compared with information on assaults collected in self-report and victimization surveys over time. Confidence in recent assertions regarding levels of violence among girls is enhanced if all of these sources agree on the nature of the trends, whereas confidence is diminished if the sources disagree.

---

*Reporting agencies classify each arrest by the most serious offense charged in that arrest. If a juvenile is arrested for an aggravated assault and a simple assault, only the aggravated assault is counted in the report—the accompanying simple assault would not be represented in the data. This means that UCR data may be underrepresenting certain offenses when they are committed at the same time as more serious offenses.

Only 4 percent of juvenile arrests in 2005 were for Violent Crime Index offenses; aggravated assaults accounted for two-thirds (64 per cent) of Violent Crime Index juve nile arrests (3 percent of all juvenile arrests). Girls comprised about one- quarter (24 percent) of all juvenile arrests for aggravated assault. By contrast, simple assaults accounted for 12 percent of all juvenile arrests; other than larceny-theft and "all other offenses," simple assault was the offense for which police made the largest number of juvenile arrests (247,900). Significantly, girls account ed for one-third (33 percent) of juve nile arrests for simple assault, the largest female proportion of arrests for any type of violent crime.

Although girls comprise a smaller overall portion of juvenile arrests than boys, the two groups' arrest pat terns have diverged somewhat over the past decade. As the percentage changes in table 1 indicate, juvenile arrests generally decreased between 1996 and 2005, but the decrease was greater for boys than for girls; the exception to the general trend was arrests for simple assault, which increased for girls while decreasing for boys.[6]

Arrests for aggravated assault com prise the single largest component of the Violent Crime Index, and arrests for simple assault are the largest component of nonindex violent arrests. As shown in table 1, boys' arrests for aggravated assault decreased nearly one-quarter (–23 percent) between 1996 and 2005, while girls' arrests decreased far less (–5 percent). In contrast, girls' arrests for simple assault increased nearly one-quarter (24 percent), while boys' arrests decreased slightly (–4 percent). For Violent Crime Index offenses, arrests of males decreased more substantially (–28 percent) than did arrests of females (–10 percent). Between 1996 and 2005, the over all total of juvenile arrests dropped about 22 percent, primarily because arrests of males decreased 29 per cent, whereas arrests of females decreased 14 percent.

Table 1. Percent Change in Male and Female Juvenile Arrests for Violent Crimes, 1996–2005

Type	Girls	Boys
Aggravated assault	–5.4%	–23.4%
Simple assault	24.0	–4.1
Violent Crime Index	–10.2	–27.9
All crimes	–14.3	–28.7

Source: *Crime in the United States, 2005*—Table 33 (FBI, 2006)

Steffensmeier and colleagues (2005) assess statistically whether the gen der difference in arrest trends over the past two decades has been nar rowing, widening, or has remained essentially stable. Based on UCR arrest data from 1980 through 2003, their analysis found that the gender difference in arrest rates is essentially stable for homicide, rape, and rob bery but has narrowed considerably for aggravated assault and simple assault (Steffensmeier et al., 2005).

The gender difference for the Violent Crime Index has also narrowed significantly, but this narrowing is largely attributable to the rise in female juvenile arrest rates for aggra vated assault during the 1990s (see figure 1). If arrests for aggravated assault are omitted from the Index, the trend is essentially stable.

To better show what a narrowing or widening gender difference in vio lence means, figure 1 plots juvenile female and male arrest rate trends for aggravated assault, simple assault, and the Violent Crime Index (sum of arrests for homicide, robbery, rape, and aggravated assault), along with the female percentage of arrests, according to the UCR.

Over the past two decades, clear changes have occurred in girls' arrests and between boys' and girls' patterns of arrests in aggravated and simple assault. As figure 1 indicates, boys' and girls' arrests for aggravated assault diverged conspicuously—the female arrest rate in 2003 (88.3 girls per 100,000) was nearly double the arrest rate in 1980 (45 girls per 100,000). Although males' arrest rate for aggravated assault was five times higher than that of females, males' proportional increase from 1980 to 2003 (12.5 percent, from 239.4 to 269.5 boys per 100,000) was much more modest than that of girls.

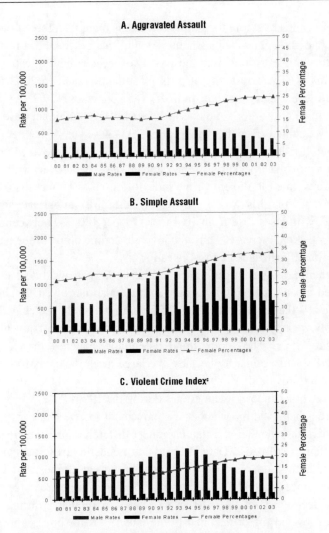

a Rates are adjusted for the gender composition of the population and for changes in
   UCR coverage over time. The population base includes ages 12–17.
b Female Percentage = Female Rate / (Female Rate + Male Rate) x 100%
c The Violent Crime Index includes homicide, aggravated assault, rape, and robbery
Source: Steffensmeier et al., 2005. Permission was given by the American Society of
   Criminology to reprint this figure, which was originally published in *Criminology*
   (Vol. 43, No. 2).

Figure 1. Trends in Juvenile Female and Male Arrest Rates[a] (per 100,000) and Juvenile
Female Percentage of Arrests[b] for Violent Offending: Uniform Crime Reports, 1980–
2003

The juvenile arrest rate for simple assaults is more than three times greater than the rate for aggravated assaults. Again, changes in the arrest rates of females for simple assault over the past two decades have greatly outpaced those of males. The arrest rate of girls for simple assault in 2003 was more than triple (3.5 times) the rate in 1980 (478.3 versus 129.7 per 100,000). Although male arrests for simple assaults started from a higher base rate, that rate barely doubled over the same period (934.4 versus 462.7 per 100,000). Arrest rates for both groups peaked in the mid-1990s, and then male rates exhibited a much sharper dropoff than female rates. Moreover, while the male juvenile arrest rate for Violent Crime Index offenses was lower in 2003 than in 1980, the rate for girls was much higher—the girls' arrest rate for Violent Crime Index offenses rose from 70.4 to 103.1 per 100,000 between 1980 and 2003, a 46-percent increase. Thus, the juvenile "crime drop" of the past decade reflects primarily changes in arrest rates for boys.

In general, the gender difference in arrests has narrowed considerably for aggravated assault and simple assault and has also narrowed for the Violent Crime Index—the female percentage of juvenile arrests held steady during the 1980s, followed by a fairly steep rise in the female share of juvenile arrests during the 1990s. The Index trend essentially matches the pat tern for aggravated assault, primarily because the large arrest volumes for aggravated assault (two-thirds of all Violent Index offenses) swamped the effects of arrest trends in the other Index violent crimes during the 1990s.

Figure 1 helps clarify whether the movement in arrest rates is similar for both genders and whether sub stantial gender differences in juvenile arrests for violent offenses still exist. Data indicate that trends in arrest rates are roughly similar for both genders across all violent crime cat egories, but with some divergence since the mid-1990s. For example, arrest rates rose for both boys and girls over much of the past two decades, particularly during 1986–94. Then rates leveled off or declined in the late 1990s for boys, while rates for girls merely stabilized or contin ued to inch upward. Therefore, the narrowing difference in trends (par ticularly for both types of assault) is at least partly a function of the recent downward movement in boys arrest rates for violence.

Figure 2 compares the simple/ aggravated assault arrest rate ratios (arrest rate for simple assault divided by the arrest rate for aggravated assault) over two decades for boys and girls. These ratios and changes in the ratios indicate the relative seriousness of offenses for which police have arrested juveniles. In 1980, the ratio for girls was 2.9, which means that police arrested girls for simple assault about three times as often as they arrested girls for aggra vated assault. They arrested boys for simple assault about twice (1.9 times) as often as they arrested boys for aggravated assault. By 2003, police arrested girls more than five times (5.4) as often for simple assault as for aggravated assault. By contrast, the ratio of boys' arrests for simple to aggravated assault was just over threefold (3.5). These ratios show that (1) arrests for simple assault are more common than for aggravated assault (i.e., the ratios for both boys and girls are greater than 1.0) and (2) simple assaults comprise a larger percentage of arrests for girls than for boys (i.e., the simple/aggravated assault ratios are consistently higher for girls than for boys), particularly in recent years.

These differences in ratios are partly explained by gender differences in the underlying trends for aggravated and simple assaults. The large decline in boys' arrests for aggravated assaults over the past decade raised their ratio of simple to aggravated assault. By contrast, the larger increase in the girls' ratio of simple to aggravated assault is attributable to their large increase in arrests for simple assault over the same period.

The statistics on juvenile arrests for assault point to certain con clusions about the seriousness of girls' violence, especially relative to the seriousness of boys' violence. Although juvenile arrests for assault—regardless of gender—are far more likely to involve simple assault than aggravated assault, the fact that the ratio of simple to aggra vated assault arrests is much higher for girls than boys suggests that most girls' violence is of a less serious nature than boys' violence. Moreover, one of the reasons that boys are more likely than girls to be charged with aggravated assault is that boys use weapons more frequently and physically inflict more injury on their victims—both indicators of the relative seriousness of boys' versus girls' violence. Finally, although girls' rate of arrest for simple assault has increased over the decades, their arrest rate for aggravated assault has not.

Despite dramatic changes in the number and rate of arrests and in simple/aggravated assault ratios, the question remains whether these trends signify a real change in girls' underlying violent behavior or reflect other factors.

Researchers have examined the changing nature of assaults over the past decades by comparing ratios of aggravated assaults to homicides (e.g., Zimring, 1998) or ratios of assaults to robberies (e.g., Zimring and Hawkins, 1997; Snyder and Sickmund, 2000). Because arrests for assault increased without cor responding increases in arrests for homicide or robbery, these analysts attribute the increases in assault arrests to changes in law enforce ment policies, such as responses to domestic violence, rather than to actual increases in assaults. Several factors relevant to interpreting statis tics on girls' arrests for assault must be considered:

- Law enforcement policies that lower the threshold for reporting an assault or for classifying an assault as ag gravated may create the appearance of a "crime wave" when the underlying behavior remains relatively stable.
- Heightened sensitivity to domestic violence has led many States and localities to implement "manda tory arrest" policies in response to domestic disturbances. Behaviors once considered "ungovernable" (a status offense) may, in a domes tic situation, result instead in an arrest for simple assault—possibly in response to the Juvenile Justice and Delinquency Prevention Act of 2002, which requires States to decriminalize and deinstitution alize status offenses (Schneider, 1984; Mahoney and Fenster, 1982; Chesney-Lind and Sheldon, 2004; Girls Inc., 1996).
- Family dynamics may also contribute to gender differences in juvenile arrests for assault. Parents have different expectations about their sons' and daughters' obedience to parental authority (Chesney-Lind, 1988), and these expectations may affect how the justice system responds to a girl's behavior when she "acts out" within the home (Krause and McShane, 1994). Research indicates that girls fight with family members or siblings more frequently than boys, who more often fight with friends or strangers (Bloom et al., 2002). Some research suggests that girls are three times as likely as boys to assault a family member (Franke, Huynh-Hohnbaum, and Chung, 2002).
- Policies of mandatory arrest for domestic violence, initially adopted to protect victims from further attacks, also provide parents with another method for attempting to control their "unruly" daughters. Regardless of who initiates a violent domestic incident, law enforcement first responders may consider it more practical and efficient to identify the youth as the offender, especially when the parent is the caretaker for other children in the home (Gaarder, Rodriguez, and Zatz, 2004).
- It is possible that school officials' adoption of zero-tolerance policies toward youth violence may increase the number of youth referred to police for schoolyard tussles that schools previously handled internally.

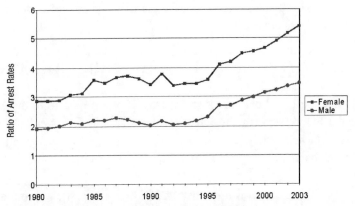

Source: National Center for Juvenile Justice (February 28, 2005), available at www.ojjdp.ncjrs.org/ojstatbb/ crime/excel/jar_20050228.xls.

Figure 2. Ratio of Simple/Aggravated Assault Rates for Juvenile Males and Females, 1980–2003

One way of assessing the "policy change hypothesis" is to compare girls' arrest trends for violent offenses to trends reflected in self-report and victimization data, using MTF and NCVS. Unlike the UCR, these data are not limited to cases that come to the attention of the police or result in arrests. If higher female arrest rates for violent crime are a byproduct of policy changes, then one would expect to find disagreement between official and unofficial data sources, with arrest data showing noticeably larger gains in female violence than found in self-report or victimization data. In contrast, if higher female rates reflect true changes in the aggressive tendencies of girls, then data sources should generally be in agreement.

Trends in Self-Reported Assaults: Monitoring the Future Data

As with the UCR arrest data, Steffensmeier and colleagues (2005) used MTF data from 1980 through 2003 to explore female- versus-male trends with tests to determine any statistical differences. Focusing on self-reported assaults, the researchers calculated prevalence (one or more incidents) and high frequency (five or more incidents) estimates for an assault index comprising three assault items[7] for 12th graders (ages 17–18). Data indicate marked stability in the separate trends for both boys and girls for the assault index over the 1980–2003 period, regardless of whether prevalence or high-frequency measures are used.

WHAT DO WE LEARN FROM SELF-REPORT DATA?

In contrast to official arrest statistics, self-report data from the Monitoring the Future surveys show that levels of assault for juvenile females and males have been fairly constant over the past two decades and that female involvement in violence has not increased relative to male violence.

These statistical patterns are illustrated in figure 3 (p. 8), where the trends over the past two decades show overall stability (i.e., random fluctuations rather than any consistent upward or downward trend). Assault rates among both girls and boys are relatively unchanged over this period, although female assault levels are consistently lower than male levels for both prevalence and high-frequency measures. Also, the gender difference in high-frequency violent assaults is quite large: Girls account for an average of about 15 percent of high-frequency assaults, compared with about 35 percent for less frequent or minor involvement in violence.

Trends in Victims' Reports of Assaults: National Crime Victimization Survey Data

Steffensmeier and colleagues (2005) also analyzed NCVS data to explore trends in assault and violence as reported by victims. Again, their analy sis relies on statistical tests and illustra tive plots of female- versus-male trends during 1980–2003. The results indicate that the rates of violence among adolescent females relative to rates among adolescent males have changed very little during this period (i.e., year-to-year changes in female versus-male rates are not statistically significant). This is true for violent offenses in general and assault in particular. The trends for both aggravated assault and simple assault are stable, a pattern contrary to UCR arrest trends, which show a narrowing gen der gap. The gender difference in NCVS trends is also stable for the Vio lent Crime Index, also contrary to the UCR trends.

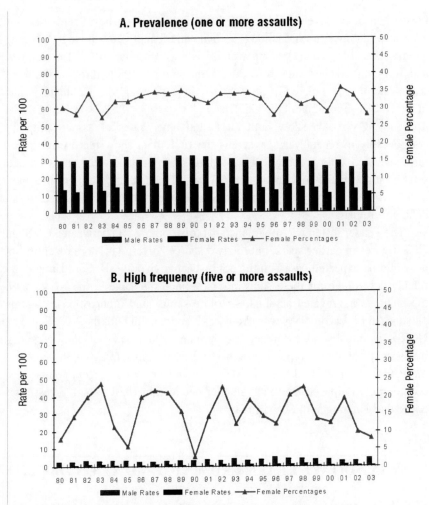

A. Prevalence (one or more assaults)

B. High frequency (five or more assaults)

* Items in the assault index include (1) hit instructor/supervisor, (2) fight at
  school/work, and (3) hurt someone badly in a fight.
Source: Steffensmeier et al., 2005. Permission was given by the American Society of
  Criminology to reprint this figure, which was originally published in *Criminology*
  (Vol. 43, No. 2).

Figure 3. Trends in Female and Male Self-Reported Assault* and Female Percentage
of Violent Offending: Monitoring the Future, 1980–2003 (17- and 18-year-olds)

Figure 4 (p. 9) illustrates these findings by showing NCVS rates of
violence for juvenile males and females (per 100,000), along with the relevant
female percentages. Based on NCVS reports, girls' violence levels are much

lower than boys' levels. Girls' rates typically rise when boys' rates rise and decline when boys' rates decline (i.e., male and female rates move in tandem), yielding a stable gender gap in overall violence. Similar to UCR data, girls' and boys' 50 assault rates rose during the late 45 1980s through the early 1990s and 40 then tapered off, but the rise is smaller and the decline is greater in the NCVS series than in the UCR series.

The NCVS data show both girls' and boys' rates of assault dropping considerably in recent years, whereas the UCR data show that assault arrest rates declined only for boys. This telling difference between the two data sources supports the conclusion that policy shifts and changes in enforce-ment may have had a greater impact on arrest rates than have actual changes in the behavior of girls.

The gender difference in violence is fairly comparable between NCVS and UCR figures in earlier years, but the two sources diverge in more recent years, as would be expected based on the policy change hypothesis. For example, the female percentage for the assault index (defined the same in the NCVS as in the UCR as aggravated assaults, simple assaults, and other offenses against persons) in the early 1980s was about 18–20 percent in both the NCVS and the UCR— essentially no difference; by the late 1990s, however, the percentage holds steady at about 20 percent in the NCVS but jumps to about 30 percent in the UCR. Sizable declines in NCVS assault rates in recent years have considerably outpaced the much smaller declines in UCR assault arrest rates, particularly among adolescent girls.

WHAT DO WE LEARN FROM VICTIMIZATION DATA?

In contrast to official arrest statistics, victimization data from the National Crime Victimization Survey show very little change in the gender gap for assault crimes and the Violent Crime Index over the past two decades and since the 1994 peak in violent crimes.

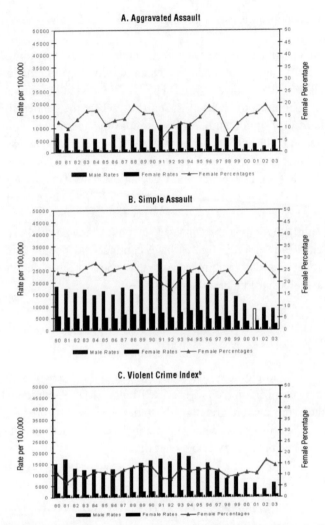

a Data are adjusted to take into account effects of the survey redesign in 1992. The multiplier is offense and sex specific and is calculated based only on juvenile data. The formula is: Multiplier = (n92 + n93 + n94)/(n90 + n91 + n92).

b The Violent Crime Index includes aggravated assault, rape, and robbery.

Source: Steffensmeier et al., 2005. Permission was given by the American Society of Criminology to reprint this figure, which was originally published in *Criminology* (Vol. 43, No. 2).

Figure 4. Trends in Juvenile Female and Male Violence Rates[a] (per 100,000) and Female Percentage of Violent Offending: National Crime Victimization Survey, 1980–2003

Several conclusions can be drawn from the NCVS data:

- First, gender differences in juvenile violent offending, including assault, have not changed meaningfully or systematically in the NCVS data since 1980. The NCVS assault finding stands in sharpcontrast to UCR arrest statistics, where the gender difference has narrowed significantly for both simple and aggravated assault.
- Second, the NCVS series reveals sharp declines in assault crimes among both girls and boys since about the mid-1990s, but girls' declines are not seen in the UCR arrest data. This discrepancy in the two data sources may be caused in part by changes in policies and practices.
- Third, these possible changes in policy are particularly salient for girls, whose arrest figures have continued to rise or barely level off compared with victim reports that show sizable declines in girls' assaults since at least the mid-1990s.

Summary

Figure 5 highlights the differences in trends between official arrest data (UCR) and victimization (NCVS) and self-report (MTF) sources. These graphs clearly show the upward trend in the female percent of arrests for assaults based on UCR arrest data, while the trends based on victimiza- tion data and self-reports have been fairly stable over time.

CONTEXT OF GIRLS' VIOLENCE

In addition to analyzing juvenile violence trends in arrests, victimiza- tion, and self-reported behavior to gain insight into female offending patterns, the Girls Study Group has explored the context in which girls exhibit violence. In a nationally representative sample, research has found that for both girls and boys, physical aggression is most common among same-sex peers, accounting for about 50 percent of incidents in which adolescents are violent (Franke et al., 2002). For girls who are physically assaultive, a family member is the second most common target (20.2 percent of girls' compared with 5.7 percent of boys' fights are with family members). The second most common target of boys' assaults is strangers. Consistent with this pattern, girls' violence more often occurs at home, whereas boys' violence more often occurs away from home. Findings that girls are particularly likely to act violently in certain settings or under certain conditions affirm the importance of examining the context of violence for insights into why girls are sometimes violent.

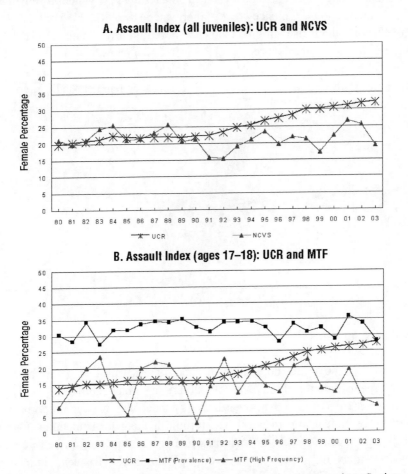

Source: Steffensmeier et al., 2005. Permission was given by the American Society of Criminology to reprint this figure, which was originally published in *Criminology* (Vol. 43, No. 2).

Figure 5. Summary of Trends in Juvenile Gender Gap for Assault in Arrest Data Compared With Victimization and Self-Report Sources: Uniform Crime Reports, National Crime Victimization Survey, and Monitoring the Future, 1980–2003

WHAT HAVE WE LEARNED ABOUT TRENDS IN GIRLS' AND BOYS' VIOLENCE?

Across all data sources, the gender difference in trends for minor kinds of violence (e.g., simple assault) is much smaller than the gender difference for more serious violence (e.g., aggravated assault). In contrast to conclusions about rises in girls' violence based on arrest statistics (UCR), the results from other sources (MTF and NCVS) show very little overall change in girls' assault levels or in Violent Crime Index offenses and essentially no change in the gender differences or femaleto-male ratio of violent offending.

Violence against Peers

Girls and boys are more likely to attack their same-sex peers than any other type of victim (Franke et al., 2002), as noted above. A study by Lockwood (1997) found that, regardless of gender, the most common reasons youth were violent toward peers was to punish them for something done or said, to get them to back down from offensive actions, and in self-defense. Physical touching, often aggressive, was the most frequent immediate precipitator of a violent incident. The second most common trigger of peer violence was negative verbal exchanges.

Other researchers have examined the relationship between physical violence and relational aggression, which includes trying to damage the social standing or self-esteem of peers by using verbal rejection, gossip, rumor spreading, and social ostracism (Cairns et al., 1989; Galen and Underwood, 1997). In some social and cultural groups, the influences against fighting weaken the connection of relational aggression to physical violence; specifically, Goodwin (1990) found that among middle-class African American youth, episodes of relational aggression were followed by nonphysical confrontations and ostracism but not by physical fighting. Corsaro and Eder (1990) found that relational aggression among economically dis advantaged girls may be more likely to escalate into physical fighting, perhaps due to a need or desire to emphasize one's own toughness and independence. Whether relational aggression leads to physical fighting may be tempered by other factors such as social class and local community and peer group norms (on peer group norms, see Crick, Bigbee, and Howe, 1996).

CONTEXT DEFINED

Context includes targets (e.g., peers, family members); specific settings (e.g., schools, neighborhoods, peer groups); and the precursors (e.g., prior victimization, relational aggression) leading up to an act of violence.

Research indicates that another factor in girls' violence against other girls involves the contradictory messages girls receive regarding sexuality. For most girls, models and images of healthy sexual desire are rare or nonexistent (Welles, 2005). Rigid imagery about "appropriate" behavior for girls can emphasize being attractive to and desired by boys and at the same time, send girls messages that they are valued for abstaining from sexual behavior. A great deal of societal emphasis is placed on being thin and looking like a supermodel or a Barbie doll (Schooler, Ward, and Merriwether, 2004; Wolf, 1991; Bordo, 1993; Davis, 1995). Artz (1997) found that the girls at risk for engaging in same-sex peer violence did not have any sense of themselves or other girls as having their own legitimate sexual desires or being valued. They understood their own sexual value only in relation to how they satisfied males and lived up to idealized standards of femininity. Thus, these girls were quick to strike out at other girls who threatened their view of self or their relationships with valued males.

Violence against Family Members

After peers, family members are the second most common target of girls' violence. Data from the FBI's National Incident-Based Reporting System for 2001 (FBI, 2003), analyzing reports of assaults by juvenile males and females by type of victim, clearly show that girls are more likely to be involved in both aggravated and simple assaults against adult family members than are their male peers, as shown in table 2 (p. 12).

When a girl uses violence against a family member, a parent—usually the mother—is the most common target.[8]

Prior victimization (in the home, in the community, or at school) appears to be a significant precursor to vio lent behavior for girls (Song, Singer, and Anglin, 1998; Molnar et al., 2005). Violence against a family member may also be a result of social learn ing that takes place when girls watch family and others who are constantly assaulting them and each other (Miller, 2001). Although girls are more likely than boys to internalize negative emotions when victimized (e.g., become depressed or anxious), they do sometimes exhibit external izing behavior, using violence in self-defense, to prevent further attack, or because they are angry.

Research indicates that in cultures that are very patriarchal and/or that devalue females, girls may be more at risk for abuse, neglect, and sexual assault (Jiwani, Janovicek, and Cameron, 2002). However, no research adequately examines whether this greater abuse or control of girls in some cultural groups translates into the girls' greater use of violence, either inside or outside the family. It is plausible that in very patriarchal families, gender-related restrictions on girls severely limit girls' use of violence and their expression of anger. A study by Heimer and DeCoster (1999) using self-report survey data showed that girls who have traditional views of gender, and, therefore, traditional views of female behavior, are less likely to engage in violence.

Violence in Schools

Although school-related deaths, violent victimizations in school, and overall school crime declined during the 1990s (Kaufman et al., 2001), public concern about school safety increased, especially in the wake of several highly publicized school shootings between 1992 and 1999 (Anderson et al., 2001). The Youth Risk Behavior Surveillance surveys (YRBSS), conducted biannually in schools in 32 States and certain localities by the Centers for Disease Control and Prevention, provide statistics regarding violent behavior by students. The 2003 survey shows that fighting is common among high school students: 33 percent of students (40.5 percent of males and 25.1 percent of females) surveyed had been in a physical fight in the last year (Grunbaum et al., 2004). Research has also shown that girls' violent delinquency is greater in middle schools than in high schools, independent of a girl's age. (Payne and Gottfredson, 2005). Further more, in 2004, 32 percent of all seri ous, violent crimes (including rape, sexual assault, robbery, or aggravated assault) against youth ages 12–18 occurred during school or on the way to and from school (Dinkes et al., 2006).

Bullying in schools appears to differ by gender. Boys are more likely to be the perpetrators and victims of direct bullying, either with physical actions or with words or gestures. Girls, in contrast, are more likely to be the perpetrators and victims of indirect bullying, or relational aggression, such as spreading rumors. In addi tion, boys are more often the perpe trators in bullying incidents in which girls were the victims (Olweus, 1993; Isernhagen Harris, 2003).

Although girls are not frequently violent in schools, when they behave violently they may do so to protect themselves. Some studies have found that girls intensify their fighting to stop their own victimization (includ ing sexual harassment) and when they feel this victimization is ignored by school officials (Brown, 1998; Belknap, Dunn, and Holsinger, 1997).

Table 2. Type of Victim in Aggravated and Simple Assaults by Boys and Girls

Type of Victim	Simple Assault		Aggravated Assault	
	Boys	Girls	Boys	Girls
Juvenile family	5%	5%	4%	7%
Juvenile acquaintance	54	49	45	40
Juvenile stranger	5	3	6	2
Adult family	17	23	12	21
Adult acquaintance	16	17	21	24
Adult stranger	4	3	12	6

Source: Information for this table was provided by Howard Snyder (Director of Systems Research at the National Center for Juvenile Justice), using data from the FBI's National Incident-Based Reporting System for 2001 (FBI, 2003).

Some teachers communicate a very restrictive standard for what is con sidered "appropriate" behavior for boys as compared with girls. When teachers hold girls and boys to different standards, they can create an atmosphere that indirectly encourages girls to use violence. Research on a school with a socially diverse student body found that teachers sometimes created a hostile environment that fed antagonisms among groups of youth (Rosenbloom and Way, 2004). In another study, some girls who perceived themselves as negatively "marked" by minority racial and socioeconomic identity maintained their status in school by not backing down when they were threatened by peers and/or when they were angry with teachers. Some also reported saving face or earning status through their prowess in fighting (Leitz, 2003).

Girls may also fight out of a sense of hopelessness. A recent ethnographic study of low-income girls in Philadel phia found that the girls thought their futures were bleak regardless of what they did at school. They felt alienated from legitimate institutions, including schools, and felt that entanglement with the law could not make things worse (Ness, 2004).

Poverty and Disorganized Communities

Poverty concentrates mothers and their children in neighborhoods characterized by few legitimate opportunities to earn money, a prevalence of illegitimate opportunities, and limited and strained public health, mental health, educational, and recreational resources. Several studies have found a link between exposure to violence in disorganized communities and youth's use of violence (DuRant et al., 1994; Burman, 2003; Fitzpatrick, 1997). A recent longitudinal study (Molnar et al., 2005) of adolescent girls in Chicago found that girls were more likely to perpe trate violence if they had previously been victimized and if they lived in neighborhoods with a high concen tration of poverty or with high homicide rates.

A girl living in a disorganized neighborhood may be more likely to use violence for a number of reasons (Leventhal and Brooks-Gunn, 2000). In communities that lack informal institutions for monitoring and supervising youth's behavior, risk of victimization is high, and girls may be violent to prevent or stop attacks on themselves (Leitz, 2003). Parents who are themselves coping with structurally disadvantaged neigh borhoods and poverty may lack the capacity to buffer the negative environment for their daughters by, for example, providing close monitoring or safe places for recreation and socializing. In such communities, schools and recreational activities often do not provide safe places for youth, leaving girls to their own devices to establish status among peers and to prevent and counteract violence against themselves. As discussed earlier, willingness to fight and prowess in fighting are two of the few ways that youth feel they can gain status in communities with few opportunities to develop talents or succeed in school. Status may be enhanced for girls who are willing to fight, because these girls are valuable to friends who might need protection and also because they can protect themselves (Jones, 2004; Ness, 2004).

A girl's physical maturity may place her at special risk in disorganized neighborhoods. Girls with early-onset puberty who live in neighborhoods of highly concentrated disadvantage are at significantly greater risk for violent behaviors when compared to early-maturing girls who live in less disadvantaged neighborhoods (Obeidallah et al., 2004). This finding has several possible explanations. Early-maturing girls who live in disadvantaged neighborhoods may be particularly prone to affiliate with delinquent peers (Ge et al., 2002). These girls might become involved with older boys who are attracted to them, and the older boys might model and encourage girls' use of violence (Ge et al., 2002). Some studies suggest that girls with boyfriends who live in disorganized or poor communities may be more likely to engage in fighting to keep the boy friend, who may provide important material or financial support (Ness, 2004). Finally, early-maturing girls may become involved with gangs and other negative peers in reaction to parental efforts to protect them by keeping them at home (Haynie, 2003).

Girls and Gangs

A very specific aspect of the context in which girls may exhibit violence is their involvement in gangs. Because research relevant to understanding girls' involvement in gangs is diverse, this section offers an overview in three parts: membership, delinquen cy, and risk factors.

Membership

Researchers have derived estimates of girls' membership in gangs from official data sources and self-report surveys. In addition to estimating the prevalence of girls' membership, research has also examined the gender composition of gangs.

Data from official sources sometimes underestimate the extent of girls' gang membership, especially when contrasted with self-report data. For instance, Curry, Ball, and Fox (1994) found that in some jurisdictions, law enforcement policies officially exclude females from counts of gang members. Controlling for data from these cities, the researchers still found that girls represented only 5.7 percent of gang members known to law enforcement agencies.

Underestimation of girls' gang involvement based on official reports may also be partly attributable to male gang members' greater likeli hood of being involved in serious crime, as well as to differences in average age of males and females in gangs (Bjerregaard and Smith, 1993; Fagan, 1990). Boys are more likely than girls to remain gang involved into young adulthood; for girls, gang membership is much more likely to be limited to the adolescent years (Hunt, Joe-Laidler, and MacKenzie, 2005; Miller, 2001; Moore and Hagedorn, 1996). These gender-related variations may increase the likelihood that male gang members will come to the attention of police more often than female gang members (Curry, 1999; Esbensen and Winfree, 1998).

On the other hand, results from youth surveys indicate that girls' gang involvement is only slightly below that of boys, particularly in early adolescence. For instance, find ings from the Rochester Youth Development Study, based on a stratified sample of youth in high-risk, high-crime neighborhoods, found that approximately the same percentage of girls (29.4 percent) and boys (32.4 percent) claimed gang membership when self-definition[9] was used as a measure (Thornberry et al., 2000). Evidence from this longitudinal study also suggests that girls' gang involvement tends to be of a shorter duration than boys', with girls' peak gang involvement around eighth and ninth grades.

In research based on youth surveys, estimates of girls' share of total gang membership range from 20 percent to 46 percent (Esbensen and Huizinga, 1993; Esbensen and Winfree, 1998; Fagan, 1990; Moore, 1991; Winfree et al., 1992), with wide variations from gang to gang. When female gang members in Columbus, OH, and St. Louis, MO, were asked what percentage of their gang's members were girls, answers ranged from 7 percent to 75 percent; the vast majority were in predominantly male gangs (Miller, 2001). In a survey of 366 gang members (Peterson, Miller, and Esbensen, 2001), 84 percent of males and 93 percent of females said their gangs had both male and female members. Approximately 45 percent of the male gang members and 30 percent of the females described their gangs as having a majority of male members, and 38 percent of males and 64 percent of females said their gangs had "fairly equal" numbers of males and females. Several studies suggest that the gender composition of gangs has a significant impact on the nature of gang members' activities, including their involvement in delinquency (Joe-Laidler and Hunt, 1997; Peterson, Miller, and Esbensen, 2001; Miller, 2001).

Delinquent Activity

Girls' gang-related delinquency appears to be strongly associated with the gender organization of their groups. Fleisher and Krienert (2004) suggest that having a sizable proportion of males in their social networks increases young women's participation in delinquency and violence (see also Miller and Brunson, 2000). Peterson, Miller, and Esbensen (2001), examining delinquent activity among members of gangs classified by gender composition, found that delinquency, particularly of a serious nature, was less characteristic of primarily female gangs than of primarily male, all-male, or gender-balanced gangs. The same researchers, however, found significant *within-gender* differences in delinquency rates for both girls and boys across the gang gender-composition categories (e.g., girls in primarily female gangs had the lowest rates of delinquency, but girls in majority- male gangs had higher rates of delinquency than boys in all-male gangs).

Gang-involved girls tend to participate in different types of activities than gang-involved boys. One study (Miller, 2001) found that most gang-involved young women did not participate routinely in the most serious forms of gang crime, in part because male members excluded them from these activities, but also because many of the young women chose not to be involved in activities they considered dangerous or morally troubling. Other researchers attribute differences in the delinquent activities of gang-involved girls and gang-involved boys to gender differences in norms supportive of violence and delinquency (Joe and Chesney-Lind, 1995; see also Camp-bell, 1993).

Risk Factors

Researchers often have focused on the extent to which community disorganization may have contributed to the growth of gangs in many cities.[10] These researchers suggest that inner-city youth join gangs as a way of adapting to oppressive living conditions imposed by their environments (see Hagedorn, 1998; Huff, 1989; Klein, 1995). A few studies have linked these conditions specifically to female gang involvement. For example, findings from the Rochester Youth Development Study suggest that growing up in disorganized, violent neighborhoods is a risk factor for gang involvement among young women (Thornberry, 1997). Gangs may help young women survive in these neighborhoods by teaching them how to protect themselves (Fishman, 1995) and by offering protection and retaliation (Miller, 2001).

GIRLS AND GANGS

Most research on girls and gangs focuses on amounts of gang involvement (over time and relative to boys) or the factors associated with gang involvement. Very little research has examined girls' violence within gangs. The research that has been done shows that boys in gangs are more violent than girls in gangs. Still, girls in gangs are more likely to be delinquent and violent than girls who are not in gangs. Peers, families, and neighborhoods have intersecting influences when girls become involved with gangs.

Several studies have explored the relationship between gang involvement and the family. In a study of gangs in Kansas City, MO, Fleisher (1998) documents intergenerational patterns of abuse and neglect, exac erbated by poverty and abject neighborhood conditions, which Fleisher suggests are at the heart of the gang problem (see also Campbell, 1984; Fleisher and Krienert, 2004). Moore (1991) also documents a myriad of family problems that contribute to the likelihood of gang involvement and concludes that young female gang members are especially likely to come from deeply troubled families. Female gang members are significantly more likely than male gang members (Moore, 1991) and at-risk nongang girls (Miller, 2001) to say they have experienced multiple family problems.

The ways in which family problems influence girls' gang involvement are varied, but they share a common thread: because of difficulties and dangers at home, girls began spending time away from home and meeting their social and emotional needs elsewhere. Researchers studying both male and female gang members have suggested the idea of the gang as a surrogate family for adolescents who do not see their own families as meeting their needs for belonging, nurturance, and acceptance (Huff, 1993; see also Campbell, 1990, and Joe and Chesney-Lind, 1995). In a gang, girls may find a network of friends who serve as a support system for coping with life problems (Fleisher and Krienert, 2004; Joe and Chesney-Lind, 1995).

Qualitative studies of risk factors for girls' involvement in gangs have focused on the influence of com munity conditions and family problems. Some survey-based studies, however, note various school-related attitudes and individual behaviors as risk factors or corre lates for girls' involvement in gangs. School-related attitudes include low expectations for completing school (Bjerregaard and Smith, 1993; Bowker and Klein, 1983; Thornberry, 1997), lack of school commitment (Esbensen and Deschenes, 1998), and negative attitudes toward school (Thornberry, 1997). Individual char-acteristics/behaviors include commitment to negative peers (Esbensen and Deschenes, 1998); delinquency, drug use, and positive values about drugs (Thornberry, 1997); and delinquent peers and early onset of sexual activity (Bjerregaard and Smith, 1993).

CONCLUSIONS

What We Know About Girls and Violence

Trends
Available evidence based on arrest, victimization, and self-report data suggests that although girls are cur rently arrested more for simple assaults than previously, the actual incidence of their being seriously violent has not changed much over the last two decades. This suggests that increases in arrests may be attribut able more to changes in enforcement policies than to changes in girls' behavior. Juvenile female involvement in violence has not increased relative to juvenile male violence. There is no burgeoning national crisis of increasing serious violence among adolescent girls.

Context
Although more information is needed, current literature suggests that girls' violence occurs in the following situations, for the following reasons:

- **Peer violence.** Girls fight with peers to gain status, to defend their sexual reputation, and in self-defense against sexual harassment.

- **Family violence.** Girls fight more frequently at home with parents than do boys, who engage more frequently in violence outside the household. Girls' violence against parents is multidimensional: for some, it represents striking back against what they view as an overlycontrolling structure; for others, it is a defense against or an expression of anger stemming from being sexually and or physically abused by members of the house hold.

- **Violence within schools.** When girls fight in schools, they may do so as a result of teacher labeling, in self-defense, or out of a general sense of hopelessness.

- **Violence within disadvantaged neighborhoods.** Girls in disadvantaged neighborhoods are more likely to perpetrate violence against others because of the increased risk of victimization (and the resulting violent self-defense against that victimization), parental inability to counteract negative community influences, and lack of opportuni ties for success.

- **Girls in gangs.** Survey research has shown a number of factors associated with girls' involvement in gangs (e.g., attitudes toward school, peers, delinquency, drug use, and early sexual activity); qualitative research points to the role of disadvantaged neighbor hoods and families with multiple problems (violence, drug and alcohol abuse, neglect). Girls asso ciated with primarily male gangs exhibit more violence than those in all-female gangs. Girls in gangs are more violent than other girls but less violent than boys in gangs.

What We Need To Know

Available evidence strongly sug gests that girls are, over time, being arrested more frequently for simple assaults, despite evidence from longitudinal self-report and victimization surveys that they are not actually more violent. The reasons for increasing arrests, however, are not well established. Studies of police and court practices—particularly with regard to girls—are sorely needed. Evaluations of domestic violence laws and zero-tolerance school policies and enforcement practices are also crucial.

It is also important to develop a better understanding of the con sequences for girls of increased involvement in the juvenile justice system. Longitudinal studies of girls who are arrested for assaultive behavior would help us better understand the pathways to and consequences of arrests for violent behavior among girls.

Although there does not appear to be a large increase in physical violence committed by girls, some girls do engage in violent behavior, and it is important to understand the context in which such violence occurs and how these situations differ for girls and boys. Although peers and family members are the most common tar gets of violence by girls, not all family or peer conflicts result in physical assault. Understanding which ones do, and why, remains vital for both prevention and intervention efforts.

REFERENCES

Anderson, M., Kaufman, J., Simon, T., Barrios, L., Paulozzi, L., Ryan, G., Hammond, R., Modzeleski, W., Feucht, T. & Potter, L. (2001). the School- Associated Violent Deaths Study Group.. School-associated violent deaths in the United States, 1994–1999. *Journal of the American Medical Association, 286*, 2695-2702.

Artz, S. (1997). On becoming an object. *Journal of Child and Youth Care, 11(2)*, 17-37.

Belknap, J., Dunn, M. & Holsinger, K. (1997). *Moving Toward Juvenile Justice and Youth-Serving Systems That Address the Distinct Experience of the Adolescent Female.* Gender Specific Work Group Report to the Governor. Columbus, OH: Office of Criminal Justice Services.

Benson, M. L., Fox, G. L., DeMaris, A. & Van Wyk, J. (2003). Neighborhood disadvantage, individual economic distress and violence against women in intimate relationships. *Journal of Quantitative Criminology, 19*, 207-235.

Bjerregaard, B. & Smith, C. (1993). Gender differences in gang participa tion, delinquency, and substance use. *Journal of Quantitative Criminology, 4*, 329-355.

Bloom, B., Owne, B., Deschenes, E. & Rosenbaum, J. (2002). Improving juvenile justice for females: A state wide assessment in California. *Crime & Delinquency, 4*, 526-552.

Bordo, S. (1993). *Unbearable Weight: Feminism, Western Culture and the Body.* Berkeley, CA: University of California Press.

Bowker, L. H. & Klein, M. W. (1983). The etiology of female juvenile delinquency and gang membership: A test of psychological and social structural explanations. *Adolescence, 18*, 739-751.

Brown, L. M. (1998). *Raising Their Voices: The Politics of Girls' Anger.* Cambridge, MA: Harvard University Press.

Browne, K. D. & Hamilton, C. E. (1998). Physical violence between young adults and their parents: Asso ciations with a history of child mal treatment. *Journal of Family Violence, 13(1)*, 59-79.

Burman, M. (2003). Challenging con ceptions of violence: A view from the girls. *Sociology Review, 13(4)*, 2-6.

Cairns, R. B., Cairns, B. D., Neckerman, H. J., Ferguson, L. L. & Gariépy, J. L. (1989). Growth and aggression: Child hood to early adolescence. *Developmental Psychology, 25*, 320-330.

Campbell, A. (1984). *The Girls in the Gang.* New York, NY: Basil Blackwell.

Campbell, A. (1990). Female partici pation in gangs. In *Gangs in America*, edited by C. Ronald Huff. Newbury Park, CA: Sage Publications, 163-182.

Campbell, A. (1993). *Men, Women and Aggression.* New York, NY: Basic Books.

Chesney-Lind, M. (1988). Girls and status offenses: Is juvenile justice still sexist? *Criminal Justice Abstracts, 20*, 144-165.

Chesney-Lind, M. & Sheldon, R. (2004). *Girls, Delinquency, and Juvenile Justice.* 2d ed. Belmont, CA: Thompson/Wadsworth.

Corsaro, W. A. & Eder, D. (1990). Children's peer cultures. *Annual Review of Sociology, 16*, 197-220.

Crick, N. R., Bigbee, M. A. & Howe, C. (1996). Gender differences in children's normative beliefs about aggression: How do I hurt thee? Let me count the ways. *Child Development, 67*, 1003-1014.

Curry, G. D. (1999). Race, ethnicity and gender issues in gangs: Reconciling police data. In *Problem-Oriented Policing: Crime-Specific Issues and Making POP Work,* Volume II, edited by C.S. Brito and T. Allan, Washing ton, DC: Police Executive Research Forum, 63-89.

Curry, G. D., Ball, R. A. & Fox, R. J. (1994). *Gang Crime and Law Enforce-ment Recordkeeping.* Research in Brief. Washington, DC: U.S. Depart ment of Justice, *Office of Justice Pro grams*, National Institute of Justice.

Davis, K. (1995). *Reshaping the Female Body: The Dilemma of Cosmetic Sur-gery.* New York, NY: Routledge.

Devoe, J. F., Peter, K., Kaufman, P., Ruddy, S. A., Miller, A. K., Planty, M., Snyder, T. D. & Rand, M. R. (2003). *Indicators of School Crime and Safety: 2003.* (NCJ 201257). Washington, DC: U.S. Departments of Education and Justice, *National Center for Educa tion Statistics and Bureau of Justice Statistics.*

Dinkes, R., Cataldi, E. F., Kena G. & Baurn, K. (2006). *Indicators of School Crime and Safety 2006.* Washington, DC: U.S. Departments of Education and Justice, *National Center for Edu cation Statistics and Bureau of Justice Statistics.*

DuRant, R., Cadenhead, C., Pendergrast, R. A., Slavens, G. & Wand Linder, C. (1994). Factors associ ated with the use of violence among urban black adolescents. *American Journal of Public Health*, *84*, 612-617.

Egley, A., Jr. & Major, A. K. (2004). *Highlights of the 2002 National Youth Gang Survey*. Fact Sheet. Washing ton DC: U.S. Department of Justice, Office of Justice Programs, Office of Juvenile Justice and Delinquency Prevention.

Esbensen, F. A. & Deschenes, E. P. (1998). A multi-site examination of gang membership: Does gender matter? *Criminology*, *36*, 799-828.

Esbensen, F. A. & Huizinga, D. (1993). Gangs, drugs, and delinquency in a survey of urban youth. *Criminology*, *31*, 565-589.

Esbensen, F. A., Huizinga, D. & Weiher, A. W. (1993). Gang and non- gang youth: Differences in explana tory factors. *Journal of Contemporary Criminal Justice*, *9*, 94-116.

Esbensen, F. A. & Winfree, L. T. (1998). Race and gender differences between gang and nongang youth: Results from a multisite survey. *Justice Quarterly*, *15*, 505-525.

Fagan, J. (1990). Social processes of delinquency and drug use among urban gangs. In *Gangs in America*, edited by C.R. Huff. Newbury Park, CA: Sage Publications, 183-219.

Federal Bureau of Investigation. (2003). *National Incident-Based Report-ing System Master File* for the year 2001 [machine-readable data files]. Washington, DC: U.S. Department of Justice, FBI.

Federal Bureau of Investigation. (2004). *Uniform Crime Reporting Handbook*. Washington, DC: U.S. Department of Justice, FBI.

Federal Bureau of Investigation. (2006). *Crime in the United States, 2005: Uniform Crime Reports*. Washington, DC: U.S. Department of Justice, FBI.

Fishman, L. T. (1995). The vice queens: An ethnographic study of black female gang behavior. In *The Modern Gang Reader*, edited by M. W., Klein, C. L. Maxson, & J. Miller. Los Angeles, CA: Roxbury Publishing Co., 83-92.

Fitzpatrick, K. M. (1997). Aggression and environmental risk among low-income African-American youth. *Journal of Adolescent Health*, *21*, 172-178.

Fleisher, M. S. (1998). *Dead End Kids: Gang Girls and the Boys They Know*. Madison, WI: University of Wisconsin Press.

Fleisher, M. S. & Krienert, J. L. (2004). Life-course events, social net works, and the emergence of vio lence among female gang members. *Journal of Community Psychology, 32,* 607-622.

Franke, T. M., Huynh-Hohnbaum, A. L. T. & Chung, Y. (2002). Ado lescent violence: With whom they fight and where. *Journal of Ethnic & Cultural Diversity in Social Work, 11(3-4),* 133-158.

Gaarder, E., Rodriguez, N. & Zatz, M. S. (2004). Criers, liars, and manipu lators: Probation officers' views of girls. *Justice Quarterly, 21,* 547-578.

Galen, B. R. & Underwood, M. K. (1997). A developmental investiga tion of social aggression among children. *Developmental Psychology, 33,* 589-600.

Ge, X., Brody, G. H., Conger, R. D., Simons, R. L. & Murray, V. M. (2002). Contextual amplification of pubertal transition effects on deviant peer affiliation and externalizing behavior among African American children. *Developmental Psychology, 38,* 42-54.

Girls Inc. (1996). *Prevention and Parity: Girls in Juvenile Justice.* Indianapolis, IN: Girls Incorporated.

Goodwin, M. H. (1990). *He-Said-SheSaid: Talk as Social Organization Among Black Children.* Bloomington, IN: Indiana University Press.

Gottfredson, G. D. & Gottfredson, D. C. (1985). *Victimization in Schools.* New York, NY: Plenum.

Grunbaum, J. A., Kann, L., Kinchen, S., Ross, J., Hawkins, J., Lowry, R., Harris, W. A., McManus, T., Chyen, D. & Collins, J. (2004). Youth risk behav ior surveillance—United States, 2003. In *Surveillance Summaries,* May 21. *Morbidity and Mortality Weekly Report, 53,* SS-2, 1-96.

Hagedorn, J. M. (1998). *People and Folks: Gangs, Crime and the Underclass in a Rustbelt City.* 2d ed. Chicago, IL: Lakeview Press.

Haynie, D. (2003). Contexts of risk? Explaining the link between girls' pubertal development and their delinquency involvement. *Social Forces, 82(1),* 355-397.

Heimer, K. & DeCoster, S. (1999). The gendering of violent delinquen cy. *Criminology, 37,* 277-317.

Huff, C. R. (1989). Youth gangs and public policy. *Crime and Delinquency, 35,* 524-537.

Huff, C. R. (1993). Gangs in the United States. In *The Gang Intervention Handbook,* edited by A. P. Goldstein, & C. R. Huff. Champaign, IL: Research Press, 3-20.

Hunt, G., Joe-Laidler, K. & MacKenzie, K. (2005). Moving into motherhood: Gang girls and controlled risk. *Youth & Society, 36,* 333-373.

Isernhagen, J. & Harris, S. (2003). A comparison of ninth- and tenth-grade boys' and girls' bullying behav ior in two states. *Journal of School Violence, 2(2)*, 67-80.

Jiwani, Y., Janovicek, N. & Camer on, A. (2002). Erased realities: The vio lence of racism in the lives of immi grant and refugee girls of colour. In *In the Best Interests of the Girl Child, Phase II Report*, edited by H. Berman and Y. Jiwani. Ottawa, Canada: Alli ance of Five Research Centres on Vio lence, Status of Women in Canada, 45-88.

Joe, K. A. & Chesney-Lind, M. (1995). "Just Every Mother's Angel": An anal ysis of gender and ethnic variations in youth gang membership. *Gender & Society, 9*, 408-430.

Joe-Laidler, K. & Hunt, G. (1997). Violence and social organization in female gangs. *Social Justice, 24*, 148-169.

Jones, N. (2004). "It's not where you live, it's how you live": How young women negotiate conflict and vio lence in the inner city. *Annals of the Academy of Political and Social Science, 595*, 49-62.

Kaufman, P., Xianglei, C., Choy, S., Peter, K., Ruddy, S., Miller, A., Fleury, J., Chandler, K., Planty, M. & Rand, M. (2001). *Indicators of School Crime and Safety: 2001*. Washington, DC: U.S. *Departments of Education and Justice*, National Center for Educa tion Statistics and Bureau of Justice Statistics.

Klein, M. W. (1995). *The American Street Gang: Its Nature, Prevalence and Control*. New York, NY: Oxford University Press.

Krause, W. & McShane, M. (1994). A deinstitutionalization retrospective: Relabeling the status offender. *Journal of Crime and Justice, 17*, 45-67.

Leitz, L. (2003). Girl fights: Exploring females' resistance to educational structures. *International Journal of Sociology and Social Policy, 23(11),* 15-43.

Leventhal, T. & Brooks-Gunn, J. (2000). The neighborhoods they live in: The effects of neighborhood residence on child and adolescent outcomes. *Psychological Bulletin, 126(2)*, 309-337.

Lockwood, D. (1997). *Violence Among Middle School and High School Students: Analysis and Implications for Prevention*. Research in Brief. Washington, DC: U.S. Department of Justice, Office of Justice Programs, National Institute of Justice.

Mahoney, A. R. & Fenster, C. (1982). Female delinquents in a suburban court. In *Judge, Lawyer, Victim and Thief: Women, Gender Roles and Criminal Justice,* edited by N. H. Rafter, & E. A. Stanko, Boston, M A: Northeastern University Press.

Miller, J. (2001). *One of the Guys: Girls, Gangs and Gender.* New York, NY: Oxford University Press.

Miller, J. & Brunson, R. K. (2000). Gender dynamics in youth gangs: A comparison of male and female accounts. *Justice Quarterly, 17(3),* 801-830.

Molnar, B. E., Browne, A., Cerda, M. & Buka, S. L. (2005). Violent behavior by girls reporting violent victimiza tion. *Archives of Pediatric and Adolescent Medicine, 159,* 731-39.

Moore, J. (1991). *Going Down to the Barrio: Homeboys and Homegirls in Change.* Philadelphia, PA: Temple University Press.

Moore, J. & Hagedorn, J. (1996). What happens to girls in the gang? In *Gangs in America,* 2d ed., edited by C.R. Huff. Thousand Oaks, CA: Sage Publications, 205-218.

Ness, C. D. (2004). Why girls fight: Female youth violence in the inner city. *Annals of the American Academy of Political and Social Science, 595,* 32-48.

Obeidallah, D., Brennan, R. T., Brooks- Gunn, J. & Earls, F. (2004). Links between pubertal timing and neigh borhood contexts: Implications for girls' violent behavior. *Journal of the American Academy of Child and Adolescent Psychiatry, 43(12),* 1460-1468.

Olweus, D. (1993). *Bullying at School: What We Know and What We Can Do.* Oxford, England: Blackwell.

Payne, A. A. & Gottfredson, D. C. (2005). Gender- and race-based out comes in the effect of school-related factors on delinquency and victim ization. Unpublished manuscript.

Peterson, D., Miller, J. & Esbensen, F. A. (2001). The impact of sex compo sition on gangs and gang member delinquency. *Criminology, 39(2),* 411-439.

Rosenbloom, S. R. & Way, N. (2004). Experiences of discrimination among African American, Asian Ameri can, and Latino adolescents in an urban high school. *Youth & Society, 35(4),* 420-451.

Scelfo, J. (2005). Bad girls go wild. *Newsweek* (June 13). [Available online at http://www.msnbc.msn.com/ id/8101517/site/newsweek/page/2/.]

Schneider, A. L. (1984). Divesting sta tus offenses from juvenile court jurisdiction. *Crime and Delinquency, 30,* 347-370.

Schooler, D., Ward, L. M. & Merriwether, A. (2004). Who's that girl: Television's role in the body image development of young white and black women. *Psychology of Women Quarterly, 28,* 38-47.

Snyder, H. forthcoming. *Juvenile Arrests* (2005). Bulletin. Washington, DC: U.S. Department of Justice, Office of Justice Programs, Office of Juvenile Justice and Delinquency Prevention.

Snyder, H. & Sickmund, M. (2000). *Challenging the Myths.* Bulletin. Washington, DC: U.S. Department of Justice, Office of Justice Programs, Office of Juvenile Justice and Delin quency Prevention.

Song, L., Singer, M. I. & Anglin, T. M. (1998. Violence exposure and emotional trauma as contributors to adolescents' violent behaviors. *Archives of Pediatric and Adolescent Medicine* 152,531-536.

Steffensmeier, D., Schwartz, J., Zhong, S. H. & Ackerman, J. (2005). An assessment of recent trends in girls' violence using diverse longitu dinal sources: Is the gender gap closing? *Criminology, 43(2)*, 355-406.

Straus, M. A. & Gelles, R. J. (1990). How violent are American families?: Estimates from the National Family Violence Resurvey and other stud ies. In *Physical Violence in American Families: Risk Factors and Adaptations to Violence in 8,145 Families,* edited by M.A. Straus and R.J. Gelles. New Brunswick, NJ: Transaction Books, 95-112.

Thornberry, T. P. (1997). Membership in youth gangs and involvement in seri ous and violent offending. In *Serious and Violent Juvenile Offenders: Risk Factors and Successful Interventions,* edited by R. Loeber and D.P. Far rington. Thousand Oaks, CA: Sage Publications, 147-166.

Thornberry, T. P., Krohn, M. P., Lizotte, A. J., Smith, C. A. & Tobin, K. (2000). *Gangs in Developmental Perspective: The Origins and Consequences of Gang Membership.* Washington, DC: U.S. Department of Justice, Office of Juvenile Justice and Delinquency Prevention.

Welles, C. E. (2005). Breaking the silence surrounding female ado lescent sexual desire. *Women and Therapy, 28*, 31-45.

Winfree, L. T., Jr., Fuller, K., Vigil, T. & Mays, G. L. (1992). The definition and measurement of "gang status": Policy implications for juvenile jus tice. *Juvenile and Family Court Journal, 43*, 29-37.

Wolf, N. (1991). *The Beauty Myth: How Images of Beauty Are Used Against Women.* New York, NY: Anchor Books.

Worcel, S. D., Shields, S. A. & Pat erson, C. A. (1999). "She looked at me crazy": Escalation of conflict through telegraphed emotion. *Adolescence, 34*, 689-697.

Zimring, F. E. (1998). *American Youth Violence.* New York, NY: Oxford University Press.

Zimring, F. E. & Hawkins, G. (1997). *Crime Is Not the Problem: Lethal Violence in America.* New York, NY: Oxford University Press.

ACKNOWLEDGMENTS

The Girls Study Group is a group of multidisciplinary experts who have been convened to assess current knowledge about the patterns and causes of female delinquency and to design appropriate intervention programs based on this information.

This Bulletin was compiled by Margaret A. Zahn (Principal Investigator of the Girls Study Group project) and Susan Brumbaugh, with the assistance of Tara Williams, and is based on excerpts from manuscripts written for the Girls Study Group by the following authors:

- Barry Feld[*] and Darrell Steffensmeier[*]: trends (permission to use previously published material from Darrell Steffensmeier is granted by *Criminology*).
- Merry Morash[*] and Meda Chesney-Lind[*]: context.
- Allison Ann Payne, Denise Gottfredson, Candace Kruttschnitt[*]: violence within schools.
- Jody Miller[*]: girls in gangs.

Additional analyses on peers were contributed by Howard Snyder, Director of Systems Research at the National Center for Juvenile Justice.

[*] Girls Study Group member.

This Bulletin was prepared under cooperative agreement number #2004–JF–FX–K001 from the Office of Juvenile Justice and Delinquency Prevention, U.S. Department of Justice.

Points of view or opinions expressed in this document are those of the author(s) and do not necessarily represent the official position or policies of OJJDP or the U.S. Department of Justice.

End Notes

[1] The MTF study is funded by the National Institute on Drug Abuse. Findings are available online at www.monitoringthefuture.org.
[2] Note that UCR data count the number of arrests, not the number of individuals arrested. An unknown number of individuals are arrested more than once during a year.
[3] The Violent Crime Index includes homicide, forcible rape, robbery, and aggravated assaults.
[4] The Property Crime Index includes burglary, larceny-theft, motor vehicle theft, and arson.

[5] Nonindex offenses are simple assault, weapons offenses, drug and liquor law violations, driv ing under the influence, disorderly conduct, vandalism, and other categories not included in the FBI's Crime Indexes. Status offenses are acts that are offenses only when committed by juveniles (e.g., running away).

[6] Aggravated assault is defined as "an unlawful attack by one person upon another for the purpose of inflicting severe or aggravated bodily injury. This type of assault usually is accompanied by the use of a weapon or by means likely to produce death or great bodily harm" (FBI, 2004, p. 23). Simple assault is defined as including "all assaults which do not involve the use of a fire arm, knife, cutting instrument, or other dangerous weapon and in which the victim did not sustain serious or aggravated injuries. Agencies must classify as simple assault such offenses as assault and battery, injury caused by culpable negligence, intimidation, coercion, and all attempts to commit these offenses" (FBI, 2004, p. 26).

[7] The 12th graders were asked how often during the past 12 months they had: (1) "hit an instructor or supervisor," (2) "gotten into a serious fight at school or at work," and (3) "hurt someone badly enough to need bandages or a doctor."

[8] Some research indicates that parents are more likely to be violent toward adolescents than adolescents are toward their parents (Browne and Hamilton, 1998; Straus and Gelles, 1990). In a survey of college students (Browne and Hamilton, 1998), 80 percent of the youth who were violent toward parents said their parents were violent toward them, whereas only 59 percent of mothers' violence and 71 percent of fathers' violence was met with or precipitated by violence from the youth.

[9] A number of scholars now use self-definition as a measure of gang membership, either alone or in conjunction with more restrictive guidelines. Some researchers suggest that only youth who are members of groups involved in illegal activities should be clas sified as gang members (see Esbensen, Huizinga, and Weihen, 1993; Esbensen and Huizinga, 1993). However, Winfree et al. (1992: 34–35) found that the "self reported definition of gang mem bership proved to be a better predictor of gang-related crime than the more restrictive defini tion," which they speculate may be a result of fringe or "wannabe" members' efforts to demonstrate gang membership. Additional evidence supporting the utility of self-definition as a measure of gang membership comes from studies that have found large and stable differences between self-identified gang members and nongang youth with regard to rates of involvement in delin quency and serious crime (see Fagan, 1990).

[10] Larger cities and suburban counties consistently account for the largest proportion (around 85 percent) of reported gang members (Egley and Major, 2004). Because research has focused on urban gangs, less is known about the social processes that explain gang formation—and girls' gang involvement—in rural and subur ban areas, although some scholars have hypothesized possible cultural diffusion processes (see Klein, 1995; Miller, 2001).

INDEX

K

L

M

T

U